Ben Greene

Moving to Las Vegas

The Insider's Guide to Moving, Living, and Thriving in The Neon City

DISCLAIMER:

While every effort has been made to ensure the accuracy and reliability of the information provided in this book, the author and publisher do not assume responsibility for any errors, omissions, or contrary interpretations of the subject matter herein. The information contained within this book is provided 'as is,' with the understanding that the author is not engaged in rendering legal, medical, counseling, or other professional services or advice.

The author has sought to present the most accurate and up-to-date information available at the time of writing. However, the dynamic nature of the topics covered means that changes, errors, or omissions may occur. The author and publisher hereby disclaim any liability to any party for any loss, damage, or disruption caused by errors or omissions, whether such errors or omissions result from negligence, accident, or any other cause.

This publication is designed to provide general information on the relocation process to, and living in, Las Vegas. It is sold with the understanding that the author is not responsible for the results of any actions taken on the basis of information in this work, nor for any errors or omissions.

Readers are encouraged to confirm the information contained herein with other sources and to seek professional advice when necessary. The intent of the author is to offer information of a general nature to help you in your quest for knowledge. In the event you use any of the information in this book for yourself, which is your constitutional right, the author assumes no responsibility for your actions.

To my family, friends, and neighbors, whose unwavering support has always been my guiding light: This book is a testament to the countless conversations, shared visions, and the love that surrounds us, even when we are miles apart.

To the dreamers, adventurers, and seekers of new beginnings, may this guide serve as your compass to the vibrant heart of Las Vegas. Here's to finding your place, making your mark, and embracing the unexpected journeys that await in the neon city. Welcome to Las Vegas, where every heart finds its home.

INTRODUCTION

WHY LAS VEGAS?

Ah, Las Vegas. The sleepless Neon City, a land of lights, sequins, and sumptuous buffets as vast as the desert horizon. You may know it as a place where fortunes are made and lost on the turn of a card, where neon dreams flicker as brightly as the 12 million lights on the Strip. But real Vegas insiders know that the city beats to a rhythm that's far more complex than the bells and whistles of a slot machine on a lucky streak, and that far from being just a destination to visit, it's actually an amazing city to live in.

MYTH-BUSTING BINGO: DEBUNKING VEGAS STEREOTYPES

Yes, there are plenty of casinos in Las Vegas, but the so-called City of Sin isn't just about chasing down lady luck. Its name is Spanish for "the meadows" (more on that later), and in addition to its breathtaking natural wonders, Vegas offers a royal flush of reasons to call it home. So first things first: let's clear up a few misconceptions about this desert oasis.

Myth #1: Las Vegas is just a destination for tourists and retirees.

Wrong, partner! Vegas is a city buzzing with young professionals, entrepreneurs, artists, and families. The tech scene is hotter than a habanero margarita; the booming Arts District is 18 blocks of pulsing creative energy; and a diverse array of schools—from innovative magnet schools to private institutions—cater to the eclectic needs of the diverse, ever-growing community (with bonus points for the rolling, bouncing tumbleweeds that kids can dodge at recess!).

Myth #2: It's hot as Hades and dry as a poker chip.

It may surprise you to learn that Nevada doesn't even rank as one of the top ten hottest states in the U.S. Sure, summer can be a scorcher, but there are plenty of entertaining, air-conditioned havens to choose from—think movie theaters, museums, and even casinos (which, you'll find out, offer a lot more than just gambling!). Las Vegas is also home to pools the size of small oceans and world-famous fountains (over a thousand at the Bellagio Hotel and Casino alone!).

Myth #3: It's expensive, like a diamond-encrusted roulette wheel.

Las Vegas may be the very definition of glitter and glitz, but the city offers its residents a surprising range of living options, from budget-friendly apartments to swanky penthouses overlooking the Strip. For the price of a Burger King blowout back home, you can eat like real royalty. And the entertainment? In addition to no-cost spectacles such as the fountains on the Strip and the city's eclectic, ubiquitous street performers, Las Vegas offers unparalleled free experiences like the Silverton Casino Hotel's 117,000-gallon aquarium, featuring tropical fish and daily, interactive mermaid swims; the Arts Factory in downtown Vegas, which allows public, indoor-and-outdoor access to over 30 artists and galleries; and the dazzling, rotating floral displays at Bellagio Conservatory & Botanical Gardens, where visitors can ramble through the (impeccably maintained and sculpted) bramble, free of charge.

THE REAL REASONS WE FALL FOR VEGAS' CHARM

Now, onto the good stuff, the reasons that make even the most skeptical soul consider trading their current digs for a pool view with a generous side of desert magic.

Freedom to be you, unfiltered and unapologetically: Vegas has an unparalleled "live and let live" attitude that welcomes every resident to become part of the diverse tapestry that makes up its population. This ain't a city that judges (unless you're there to get married by a judge, at one of its 50+ chapels). Instead, Vegas truly celebrates the full spectrum of human eccentricities and idiosyncrasies.

Second chances and fresh starts: Vegas is a city of reinvention. Maybe you're feeling creatively stunted or you're actively looking for a new gig. Perhaps you've always wanted to start your own food truck, or, say, train miniature horses at the Popovich Comedy Pet Theater. If you want to chase your dreams, or discover a new path in life, the possibilities in Vegas abound like sand in the Mojave.

Adventure at your doorstep (and beyond): Hike a canyon at sunrise, kayak on Lake Mead at sunset, catch a world-class show under the stars, then dance the night away in a club pulsating with electronic beats. In Vegas, boredom is a word we simply don't use— we never have to.

Community that feels like family: People flock to Vegas from all corners of the globe, choosing to make this one-of-a-kind, all-inclusive oasis their home. The result? An undeniable sense of community and a small-town vibe in a big city, where neighbors become friends, dog walkers swap stories, and even the grumpy cashier at the convenience store cracks a smile when you ask about his lucky number.

A city that never sleeps, so neither do your dreams: Vegas is a perpetual motion machine, a city that runs on ambition, adrenaline, and maybe a little too much caffeine. Even if you're a believer in the requisite seven to nine hours of Zzz's, the Vegas vibe is infectious— an irrepressible energy that will make you reach for the stars, feeling like anything is possible.

WHY THIS BOOK?

This book is your passport to exploring, understanding, and embracing the neon jungle that is Vegas. It's not a glossy travel brochure filled with airbrushed showgirls and promises of jackpot-fueled retirements. It's a real-talk, warts-and-all guide to navigating the labyrinth of life in this desert oasis.

We'll delve into the nitty-gritty of finding a home, whether it's a budget-friendly apartment or desert-chic bungalow. We'll crack the code of the local job market, where opportunities sprout like desert wildflowers after a rare downpour. We'll explore the hidden gems beyond the Strip—the quirky neighborhoods and vibrant communities that make Vegas more than just a playground for tourists.

But most importantly, this book is a pep talk for the adventurers, the dreamers who dare to color outside the lines. It's a roadmap for building a life as unique and dazzling as the Vegas skyline, a life where every day is a chance to roll the dice and win big.

So, whether you're a seasoned gambler or a wide-eyed newcomer, this book is your guide to the real Vegas, the heart that beats beneath the neon, the siren song that calls out, "Anything is possible, darling. Just grab your sunscreen and your sense of humor, and let's paint the desert red."

P.S. If you're still not convinced, consider this: Vegas is the only place where you can eat a five-star meal, catch a world-class Cirque du Soleil show, and witness a man in a banana suit win a million bucks on a slot machine, all before the sun sets on the horizon. Need I say more?

At the heart of my decision to write this book was a desire to share the unexpected joys and quirky discoveries that come with relocating to a city as unique as Las Vegas. My life here has been filled with moments of awe, humor, and genuine human connection, often in the most unlikely of circumstances. From practicing yoga with a room full of Elvis impersonators to hosting a neighborhood barbecue that turned into an impromptu Vegas show, each experience reveals a different and delightful facet of this vibrant city.

I wrote this guide not just as a practical tool for those planning to move here, but as a love letter to the city's eccentricities and its warm, welcoming community. My aim was to offer a glimpse into the real Vegas, the one that goes beyond its (admittedly dazzling) surface. I hope that the readers will see Las Vegas as I do—not just a tourist destination, but as a lively, dynamic place to call home.

So, what are you waiting for? Grab your cowboy hat (or your sequined evening gown, or jeans and a t-shirt), turn the page, and let's get lost in the wonderland that is Las Vegas.

Are you ready to roll the dice on your new life? Then let's do this!

P.P.S. For additional resources, tips, and local insider secrets, check out https://www.reddit.com/r/movingtovegas/ It's like having a desert-savvy best friend in your pocket, always ready to point you in the direction of the next adventure.

Now, go forth and conquer. Vegas awaits!

1.   HISTORY AND CULTURE

The Entertainment Capital of the World. Sin City. The City That Never Sleeps. Las Vegas is known by many names, some of them contradictory. For example, the Divorce Capital of the World, as some call it, is also home to the highest marriage rate in the U.S. By any name, however, Las Vegas is undeniably unique.

To understand the Neon City, we must journey back, way back, to a time before glittering lights and clinking slot machines, to a time when Las Vegas was but a whisper on the wind, a mere shimmer on the horizon.

THE EARLY DAYS: WHEN THE DESERT WAS JUST SAND

Actually, before Las Vegas became the oasis we know and love today, it wasn't so much a whisper or a shimmer as it was just—sand. Lots and lots of sand. And more sand. The area was first inhabited by the Nuwuvi, or Southern Paiute peoples, for thousands of years. Also known as Nuwu, they could never have imagined that one day, the land would be home to replicas of the Eiffel Tower and Venetian canals.

The name "Las Vegas" itself was given by a Spanish trader, Rafael Rivera, in 1829. It translates to "The Meadows," which might seem incongruous, given the amount of sand for which Vegas is famous for. But back then, its impressive groundwater made the area a welcome watering hole in the desert for those heading west—a veritable meadow.

The actual settlement of Las Vegas would not start until 1905, when it was established as a railroad town—a refueling stop for trains trundling between Los Angeles and Salt Lake City. It was officially founded on May 15, 1905, when 110 acres of land were auctioned off by the railroad company.

MOB INFLUENCE & THE BIRTH OF THE STRIP

Las Vegas's real transformation, however, began in the mid-20th century, steered by the moneyed and manicured hands of mobsters. These dapper dons of the desert saw potential in Las Vegas—not as a rail stop, but as a haven for adult entertainment, a place where the profits flowed even more freely than the drinks and gambling chips.

It was American mobster Bugsy Siegel who truly kickstarted this vision. In 1946, Siegel set a precedent for the future when he opened the Flamingo, a hotel and casino far more luxurious than anything Las Vegas had seen before. It was the beginning of what we now know as The Strip, the famous stretch of Las Vegas Boulevard where you can see the iconic "Welcome to Fabulous Las Vegas, Nevada" sign, the Ancient-Egypt-themed Luxor Hotel and Casino (modeled after the Great Pyramid of Giza), and the tallest observation wheel in the world—just to name a few of the Strip's eye-popping attractions.

NEON LIGHTS & ATOMIC SIGHTS

The post-war era heralded a boom for Las Vegas, pushing it from a town of potential to a burgeoning city of spectacle. With the introduction of the first atomic bomb tests in nearby Nevada Test Site in the 1950s, Las Vegas embraced its newfound glow-in-the-dark charm. Believe it or not, atomic bombs were actually a tourist draw for a while. Hotels hosted "bomb parties" where guests could enjoy a martini and a mushroom cloud from the comfort of their balconies—a true testament to the era's blend of dread and fascination with the atomic age.

Meanwhile, The Strip continued to grow with the addition of more resorts, each more opulent and outlandish than the last. The Sands, the Sahara, and the Riviera all opened their doors, ushering in the "Rat Pack" era—a time when famous crooner cronies Frank Sinatra, Dean Martin, and Sammy Davis Jr. ruled the roost, making Las Vegas synonymous with entertainment.

CORPORATE TAKEOVER & THE MEGA-RESORTS ERA

The golden age of mob influence waned by the late 20th century, as the Vegas baton was passed to corporate honchos. The era of the mega-resort dawned, bringing with it juggernauts like the Mirage, opened by Steve Wynn in 1989. This was quickly followed by the MGM Grand, the Luxor, and the Bellagio, each a mini-city within itself, boasting everything from lion habitats to art galleries. The Las Vegas Strip morphed into a landscape where Venice sat alongside ancient Egypt, and Paris neighbored New York City.

This corporate takeover signified a shift in Las Vegas's allure. No longer was it merely a gambler's paradise; it had become a family-friendly destination, a Disneyland where real estate ventures and stock prices had become part of the thrill.

When I was a kid, I tried to recreate the Bellagio fountains in my backyard. I was inspired by the spectacle, the grandeur. With the help of a dozen garden hoses, sprinklers, and a selection of Celine Dion hits playing at top volume, I brought Vegas to my home turf. Even my dog got in on the act, leaping through the sprinklers again and again. The "fountain" was the talk of the neighborhood—and the memory serves as a poignant and humorous reminder of Las Vegas' enduring and joyful impact.

MODERN DAY: A CITY EVER EVOLVING

Today, Las Vegas stands as a monument to human ingenuity (and perhaps our inherent love for a bit of vice). It is a city that has weathered economic downturns, changing global trends, and even a global pandemic, emerging each time like a phoenix from the ashes, albeit a flashy phoenix—you know, lots of lights, sequins, and extra feathers.

As of the year 2020, Las Vegas, that ever-twinkling city in the desert, had become the chosen abode for 641,903 souls, while its greater metropolitan realm boasted 2,227,053 inhabitants. This placed it as the 25th-most populous city in the grand old United States. And let me tell you, the diversity is as rich as the buffet spread at a Vegas wedding—40.4% of these fine residents are Caucasian, 12.9% African Americans, a vibrant 33.3% Hispanic or Latino, and 7.2% of Asian descent.

The city now attracts world-renowned chefs, hosts international sporting events, and even dabbles in the high art scene, reflecting its dynamic evolution from a humble watering hole in the desert to a global center of entertainment and culture. According to a recent Redfin report, Las Vegas has also become the third most popular metro area that home buyers are moving into, underscoring its allure not just as a tourist destination but as a sought-after place to live.

At its heart, Las Vegas remains a land of possibility, a city where dreams can, and often do, become reality. Whether you're standing beneath a perfect, half-scale replica of the Eiffel Tower or watching the world through the neon glow of a hotel window fifty stories above the city, Las Vegas insists on one thing—that you marvel at the audacity of it all. This transformation speaks to the city's unyielding capacity to reinvent itself, attracting not only those in search of entertainment but also those looking to call this vibrant city home.

EPILOGUE: THE CITY OF SECOND CHANCES

As we close this chapter on Las Vegas history, it's worth pondering the lessons this magnificent metropolis teaches us. Amidst the slot machines and roulette wheels, beyond the all-you-can-eat buffets and marquee shows, lies the heart of Las Vegas—a place of reinvention, a sanctuary for the second chance, a testament to human aspiration and perseverance.

To live in Las Vegas is to witness the apotheosis of the American Dream, warts and all. It's a city that doesn't just welcome you; it embraces your wildest imaginings and dares you to dream bigger. And in that brazen, dazzling spirit of audacity, perhaps we can all find a bit of inspiration. For in the endless desert, Las Vegas stands as a beacon, a reminder that from the seemingly barren, we can forge the spectacular.

So here's to Las Vegas, the city where the impossible is merely a starting point. May it continue to dazzle, to inspire, and to remind us that in this vast, unpredictable world, there's always room for a little more light.

2. GEOGRAPHY AND CLIMATE

When considering a move to Las Vegas, there's one unavoidable truth you'll need to acquaint yourself with: the city exists in a desert. Despite the lush-sounding reference in its name to "meadows," it is in actuality the Mojave Desert—home to some dazzling natural wonders, to be sure, but a desert nonetheless.

WELCOME TO THE MOJAVE

So, picture this: Las Vegas, the seat of Nevada's Clark County, nestled like a jewel (or a rhinestone, if you'd prefer) in the Mojave Desert, surrounded by rocky terrain and rugged mountain ranges.

Imagine elevation rising over 11,900 feet from the bustling streets of the Strip to the serene, scenic Red Rock Canyon and Mount Charleston. To the west, the Spring Mountains loom like silent guardians, while smaller ranges pop up here and there, like unexpected plot twists.

The Las Vegas Valley, meanwhile, is the main event, the reason this city exists in a desert of all places. It spans about 600 square miles, sloping gently from northwest to southeast. Downtown Las Vegas sits around 2,000 feet above sea level—so what happens in Vegas is actually happening in thin air.

And despite the dramatic desert surroundings, there are actually wetlands and a channel system known as the Las Vegas Wash. This might sound like a place where you'd take your car for a clean, but it is indeed a natural source of water—and it plays a crucial role in keeping the palm trees swaying and the golf courses green.

On clear nights, the Mojave offers a vast, brilliant sky that's more star-studded than the cast of every *Ocean's Eleven* movie, reboot, and sequel combined. But the real headliner of the Las Vegas landscape is the sun. Say hello to your new, omnipresent companion!

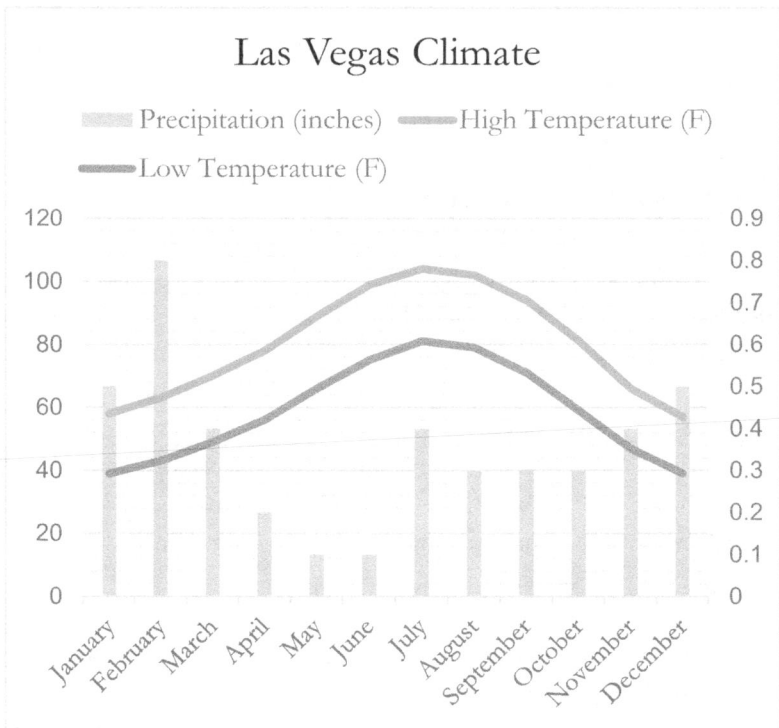

Data source: www.ncei.noaa.gov/access/us-climate-normals

A SUN-DRENCHED EXISTENCE

Las Vegas, you see, is generously sun-kissed, a polite way of saying that the sun all but governs life here. The city enjoys upwards of 310 sunny days per year. It's fantastic for your Vitamin D intake, a natural and effective mood booster, and great for fostering a close personal relationship with your air conditioner.

Summers in Las Vegas are, not to put too fine a point on it, hot. And not just any kind of hot. We're talking a "fry-an-egg-on-the-sidewalk, air-you-can-wear, stepping-into-an-oven" kind of hot. July holds court as the warmest month, with average high temperatures pirouetting around the 104°F (40°C) mark, occasionally flirting with 110°F (43°C) just for fun.

But fear not, dear transplant. Remember that Nevada isn't even one of the top ten hottest states in the U.S. (we see you, Florida!). And the desert heat is *a dry heat*—a phrase you can expect to hear more often than you ever thought possible. This is not the oppressive, sticky heat of a tropical climate (hello again, Florida!) but an all-encompassing, consistent, omnipresent warmth that seems to radiate from everywhere and nowhere all at once.

WINTER? I HARDLY KNEW HER

If you're accustomed to traditional winter weather, where snow, slush, and frozen fingertips are the norm, you are in for a real treat. Las Vegas experiences mild and remarkably brief winters, offering merely a courteous acknowledgment to the concept of "cold." From December through February, daytime temperatures average in the high 50s to low 60s°F (about 15-20°C). On the coldest winter days, daily lows can drop to around 40°F (4°C), seldom falling below 32°F (0°C). Nights are when the lows dip into chilly 30s (-1°C)

Snow is seldom seen in the city, mostly gracing the nearby Spring Mountains in a pleasantly distant and decorative fashion. Occasionally, Vegas itself receives a light dusting, an event that's greeted with a mixture of bewilderment, excitement, and the kind of mild chaos usually reserved for friendly alien invasions in movies.

I remember my first winter in Vegas. I arrived from New York City, decked out in a heavy coat, mittens, and scarf. As I stepped off the plane, I was met with sunshine and a mild, dry breeze. There I stood, dressed for an East Coast winter in a city where, a quick check of my weather app told me, it was a pleasing 60 degrees Fahrenheit. I quickly learned that in Vegas, a light jacket is more than enough to weather the winters.

SPRING AND AUTUMN: THE MOJAVE'S COURTEOUS CURTSEYS

The transitional seasons, spring and autumn, are when Las Vegas and the Mojave desert put on their best show. Temperatures are genteel, allowing for the kind of outdoor exploration that is generally warned against during the summer's furnace-like temperatures.

Spring offers a delicate bloom, a slight blush in the desert as wildflowers punctuate the landscape. It's a season of renewal, with temperatures that ascend gradually, offering a slow build to the summer's crescendo.

Autumn, conversely, is a languorous sigh of relief after the peak summer heat. The days cool off, the nights grow longer, and the entire city seems to take on a golden hue. It's the perfect time of year for exploring the surrounding desert or taking strolls along the Strip.

THE ANNUAL AFFLICTION: MONSOON SEASON

Between Vegas' mild winters and searing summers lies a period known colloquially as monsoon season. From July through September, the city can experience sudden, dramatic thunderstorms. These tempests, while infrequent, drench the desert landscape and turn the city streets into impromptu rivers.

It's a spectacle, and a reminder of nature's power. And while the rain is often welcome, it's wise to remember that flooding can, and does, occur—so familiarize yourself with flash flood response, evacuation routes, and shelter plans where applicable.

EPILOGUE: WEATHER OR NOT

Don't be daunted by the extremes of Vegas weather. Living Las Vegas means adapting: making friends with the sun (and sunscreen), staying hydrated, and keeping your air conditioner in tip-top shape. You'll learn that early mornings and late evenings are the best times for outdoor activities in the summer, with indoors being the most ideal for in-between. You'll also come to have a deep affection and appreciation for the natural wonders that accompany the Vegas weather: the vast, brilliant night skies, the unique beauty of the desert landscape, and the waterfalls that appear in Red Rock Canyon after a torrential downpour—just to name a few.

3.   ECONOMY AND EMPLOYMENT

In early 2020, the U.S. was hit hard by the economical impact of the COVID-19 pandemic—Las Vegas included. But now it's 2024, and to say that the city has bounced back is a bit of an understatement. Vegas' Gross Domestic Product (GDP) is now north of $160 billion (yep, you read that right). Nevada's economy ranks 32nd in size among states and Washington, DC. The median household income, floating just above $60,000, isn't too shabby either, especially in a state where the taxman keeps his hands mostly to himself.

The usual suspects such as tourism, conventions, entertainment, and gambling pour over $79 billion into the economy annually. But the city isn't a one-trick pony; money comes in from other industries like manufacturing, professional services, healthcare, and more. Las Vegas isn't playing cards with the economy, it's playing chess—and coming out a Grandmaster every year.

If we're using the cards analogy, however, it's safe to that on the employment front, Las Vegas is dealing out a good hand. Unemployment rates have been high, but for an unusual reason: post-pandemic, Nevada residents explored the diverse job market while relying on the money they had received via stimulus checks and unemployment benefits—in other words, as the Nevada Governor's Office of Economic Development explained to CNN in 2024, "This is an unemployment rate that's not driven by job losers, [it's] driven by job seekers." The result? Las Vegas has the sixth-fastest-growing economy in the U.S.

Moreover, Vegas just snagged the title of the 5th best city in the US for remote workers, according to data provided by the folks at Extra Space Storage—a great example of how the city is able to adapt and move forward with changing times.

Wages in Vegas are keeping up with the Joneses—or the national average, to be more precise. Service and retail workers can expect to take home $10 to $37 with an average of $20 per hour. Those in professional services and tech aren't doing too badly either, pocketing upwards of $20 to $63 an hour. And let's not forget that in Nevada, your paycheck is your own—no state income tax to nibble away at your earnings.

The following table shows the mean hourly wages for various occupations in Las Vegas. (Keep in mind, however, that just like in the casinos, where some machines pay out more than others, jobs can pay higher wages than others even for the same occupation. The mean hourly wage is a general average, not the exact amount every job pays.)

Occupation	Mean Hourly Wage
Management	$63.08
Business and financial operations	$41.39
Computer and mathematical	$51.99
Architecture and engineering	$45.52
Life, physical, and social science	$40.21
Community and social service	$26.81
Legal	$59.87
Educational instruction and library	$30.41
Arts, design, entertainment, sports, and media	$36.78

Healthcare practitioners and technical	$46.52
Healthcare support	$17.10
Protective service	$25.97
Food preparation and serving related	$15.45
Building and grounds cleaning and maintenance	$17.26
Personal care and service	$17.41
Sales and related	$24.22
Office and administrative support	$21.90
Farming, fishing, and forestry	$18.21
Construction and extraction	$28.08
Installation, maintenance, and repair	$26.77
Production	$21.81
Transportation and material moving	$21.12

Source: U.S. Bureau of Labor Statistics, Occupational Employment and Wages in Las Vegas-Henderson-Paradise, May 2022

BUSINESS CLIMATE: HIGH STAKES, HIGH REWARDS

In the complex game of business, Nevada is shuffling its deck with determination. Ranked as the 30th best state for business in 2023 by CNBC, the state is steadily climbing the business ladder. Its regulatory environment and tax structure are the business version of a warm Vegas welcome.

The Governor's Office of Economic Development isn't just rolling dice when it comes to nurturing businesses and investing in tech and energy sectors. It's more like a seasoned croupier, deftly handling tax abatements, workforce development programs, and incentives to ensure the growth of key industries. It's ensuring that businesses, big and small, find a welcoming place to thrive in Nevada.

NEON DREAMS: THE ENTERTAINMENT AND HOSPITALITY INDUSTRY

Let's start with the undeniable centerpiece of the Las Vegas economy—the gaming, entertainment, and hospitality industry. This triumvirate is the city's crowning glory, a sector that not only defines its global image but also employs a significant portion of the local workforce. From the labyrinthine casino floors to the sky-high luxury resorts, the industry is a multi-faceted gem that sparkles with opportunities for career advancement, entrepreneurship, and creativity.

The neon-soaked Strip might seem like a world of its own, but it requires a small army of workers behind the scenes to keep its glossy veneer sparkling. Employment opportunities abound in hotel management, event planning, culinary arts, and entertainment, to name but a few. It's an industry that never sleeps, demanding everything from precision to flair, from the pit boss surveying the casino floor to the cocktail mixologist crafting the next Instagram-worthy concoction.

BEYOND THE BOULEVARDS: DIVERSIFYING THE ECONOMY

In recent years, there's been a concerted effort to diversify the city's economic portfolio. Various sectors are showing robust growth, broadening the horizons for anyone looking to work and live in Las Vegas.

The leisure and hospitality sector, the backbone of Vegas, employs a small city's worth of people—around 300,000. The professional services industry employs 181,000 individuals. The education and healthcare sector and the retail sectors are not far behind, each offering jobs to about 125,000 more. Manufacturing is also getting in on the action, offering a ticket to employment for over 30,000 individuals. Farming and agriculture keeps 1,000 people busy in a city where you'd think the only crop was poker chips.

Sector	Number of Employees
Mining and logging	400
Construction	84,000
Manufacturing	32,000
Trade, transportation, and utilities	215,000
Information	13,000
Financial activities	59,000
Professional and business services	181,00
Education and health services	125,000
Leisure and hospitality	299,000
Other services	33,000
Government	115,00

Source: U.S. Bureau of Labor Statistics, Las Vegas Area Economic Summary, January 2024.

TECH TOOK A CHANCE ON VEGAS

Enter the burgeoning tech scene. Las Vegas is quickly carving out a space for itself on the digital map, with an array of startups and established tech companies setting up shop. The city's low cost of living (compared to Silicon Valley), generous tax incentives, and—let's face it—unparalleled entertainment options, make it a magnet for tech talent and entrepreneurs. It's an exciting time for innovators and IT professionals, with opportunities that span the spectrum from cybersecurity to software development.

Back in the early 2010s, Tony Hsieh, the then-head honcho of Zappos, embarked on what can only be described as a gloriously audacious venture. He transformed ordinary buses into modern-day chariots, whisking away a legion of startup founders to a somewhat forgotten corner of downtown Vegas, armed with a dream and—quite conveniently—millions of dollars. His mission? To resuscitate this sleepy district.

By 2017, his "Downtown Project" had conjured up 1,500 jobs and a staggering $210 million in economic output, though not without a spot of controversy for gently shoving some long-established locals out of the picture. Hsieh, a restless spirit, later drifted to Park City, Utah, and sadly departed our world in 2020, leaving behind his vision of a tech haven just shy of full bloom.

Yet, what he started became a veritable movement. Fast forward to 2023, and voila—Las Vegas is now the proud host to 625 startups. According to the wizards at Dealroom.co, these sprightly ventures have given jobs to over 11,000 people—that's a jump of 143.7% since 2020, if you're keeping score. Most of these techie types found homes in companies with 50 to 200 employees. And the money! In 2022, more than $4 billion flooded into these startups. Fintech enthusiasts bagged $126 million and media moguls scooped up $96.6

million, while the gaming, travel, and sports sectors were not far behind.

In a turn of events as dazzling as the city lights, a study by Crowdfund Capital Advisors (CCA) has catapulted Las Vegas to the pinnacle of startup stardom. Vaulting an impressive nine positions, this desert oasis of entrepreneurship outshone Austin, Texas to clinch the top spot in the 2023 survey, a move as surprising and spirited as Vegas itself. It seems Mr. Hsieh's half-finished dream did indeed trigger a most remarkable entrepreneurial renaissance.

WAREHOUSE WONDERS AND THE LOGISTICS LABYRINTH

Thanks to its strategic location, Las Vegas is also a hub for logistics and warehousing. The city's arteries connect to major markets across the Western United States, making it a pulsing center for distribution. Amazon and other e-commerce behemoths have massive distribution centers here, offering careers in logistics management, operations, and a variety of engineering roles. It's a sector that doesn't dazzle like a headline show, but provides the much-needed backbone to an ever-expanding online marketplace.

HEALTH AND WELLNESS: VEGAS CARES

As the population grows, so does the demand for healthcare services. Las Vegas's health and wellness sector is expanding, providing a wide array of opportunities for healthcare professionals. From hospitals to specialized clinics focusing on everything from cosmetic surgery to holistic wellness, the city is becoming a health hub for both residents and tourists seeking recovery and rejuvenation.

THE RENEWABLE REVOLUTION: CLEAN ENERGY'S BET ON NEVADA

Nevada's abundant sunshine and open landscapes make it an ideal candidate for renewable energy projects. Hoover Dam has been a longstanding source of hydroelectric power, showcasing the state's early commitment to renewable energy solutions.

Las Vegas is riding the crest of this wave, with solar energy leading the charge. Careers in clean energy range from research and development to engineering and project management, offering a bright future for those passionate about sustainability and innovation.

EDUCATION AND BUILDING THE FUTURE

With growth comes the need for educational services. Las Vegas's educational sector is expanding, with opportunities not just in teaching and administration, but also in educational technology, curriculum development, and support services. It's an area ripe for innovation, where educators have the chance to shape the future citizens and leaders of Las Vegas.

WHAT TO EXPECT: THE JOB HUNTER'S BAG OF TRICKS

If you're packing your bags and heading to Las Vegas to embark on a new career, here are a few nuggets of advice to tuck into your suitcase:

Flexibility: The most successful newcomers are those who can adapt. The city's economy is like a living, breathing organism, constantly evolving. Stay flexible and be open to opportunities in emerging sectors.

Networking Rules: Las Vegas is a city built on connections. Attend meetups, join professional associations, and don't be shy to introduce yourself— it's often who you know that opens doors to opportunities. Networking events:

- Eventbrite lists various networking events in Las Vegas, including industry-specific meetups, career fairs, and more. www.eventbrite.com/d/nv--las-vegas/networking/

- AllEvents.in features a range of business and startup entrepreneur events, seminars, and conferences in Las Vegas. These events are great for networking and learning about new opportunities. http://allevents.in/las%20vegas/business

- Las Vegas offers a vibrant array of career fair and networking opportunities for job seekers across various industries. There's the in-person Las Vegas Job Fair, which offers free career seminars and resume reviews; the Las Vegas Career Fair and Networking Event, which offers a chance to interview with leading companies; and virtual events like the Las Vegas Virtual Career Fair.

So skill up, because the competition can be fierce. Look for opportunities to upgrade your skills or learn new ones, particularly in fast-growing sectors like technology and healthcare. And utilize local resources, which are plentiful. The Nevada Department of Employment, Training and Rehabilitation (DETR) provides a wealth of information and support services for those seeking employment in Nevada. Rapid Response Services are designed to assist workers facing job loss due to economic changes, providing them with resources to find new employment swiftly. For information on obtaining Rapid Response services, call (775) 684-0362 or email rapidresponse@detr.nv.gov. DETR also maintains a presence on social media platforms and offers additional online support for job seekers and employers alike.

EPILOGUE: A CITY OF OPPORTUNITIES

Las Vegas is more than casinos and entertainment venues. It's a city on the move, expanding and evolving in exciting ways. Whether you're drawn to the high-energy hospitality industry, the innovative tech scene, the logistical marvels of warehousing and distribution, the compassionate healthcare sector, the bright future of clean energy, or the noble world of education, Las Vegas holds a promise for you. It's a city that takes chances—on people, the economy, and the future.

So, as you stand on the brink of your relocation, remember that Las Vegas is a city that bets big and wins big. It's a place where dreams are dealt like cards, and fortunes can be made in more ways than one.

4.   COST OF LIVING

When considering a move to Las Vegas, there's a lot to envision about the unique and iconic city: nighttime walks along the strip, stargazing in the desert, enjoying a poolside lemonade in the middle of the December. After all, it's a city like no other. But the underlying question about any relocation, whether it's to Vegas or West Virginia, is pretty straightforward: "What will it cost to call this place home?"

The transition to a new city invariably brings with it a tangle of financial considerations and a mix of hope for economic prosperity, as well as the dread that things might not work out. But fear not, for in this chapter we shall explore that very topic, examining Las Vegas' cost of living in comparison to other US cities—with a particular focus on practicalities such as housing, utilities, and groceries. And we've got compelling statistics to help guide us along the way.

CNN.com introduced a delightful tool, a sort of financial crystal ball if you will, designed to compare the expenses of your current abode with the potential outlays you might encounter in Las Vegas. money.cnn.com/calculator/pf/cost-of-living/index.html

A CASTLE AMIDST THE CASINOS: HOUSING IN LAS VEGAS

When you think of Las Vegas accommodations, it's easy to conjure images of ritzy hotels and room service, a lifestyle where luxury knows no bounds. Yet, for those looking to plant roots and build a home, the options are surprisingly accessible.

In contrast to the stratospheric costs of cities like New York, where the median home price hovers around $665,000 as of early 2024, or San Francisco, with a staggering median of nearly $1.3 million, Las

Vegas presents a far more practical picture. As of the same period, the median home price in Las Vegas stands at approximately $418,000. This figure reflects a market that, while competitive, remains within the realm of possibility for a broader segment of homebuyers. Given that the median household income is about $60,000, purchasing a home in Las Vegas can still pose a challenge to many—but the rental market, too, offers a range of options. The average rent for a one-bedroom apartment in Las Vegas sits around $1,362 per month, a stark contrast to the $2,891 in San Francisco or $3,343 in New York City for similar accommodations.

POWER TRIPPING: UTILITIES IN SIN CITY

So what does it cost to keep your home hospitable? Las Vegas' penchant for scorching summers means air conditioning is less a luxury and more a survival tool. This necessity is reflected in the utility bills which, during the peak summer months, can spike sharply.

On average, Las Vegas residents spend about $311 per month on electricity. That is 58% higher than the national average of approximately $196. The desert's gift of endless sunshine does, however, come with the silver lining of solar power potential, offering a possible long-term solution to lowering some of these costs.

NOURISHING THE SOUL: GROCERY TALES IN THE DESERT

There are plenty of places to buy food in Las Vegas, from farmer's markets to grocery stores and chain supermarkets. Savvy shoppers can find deals that significantly undercut the national average, but it is worth noting that in an analysis of U.S. Census Data from November 2023 by Help Advisor, the average national weekly expenditure on groceries was determined to be $270.21. (Alaska and

Hawaii were omitted from the study.) Against this backdrop, Nevada ranks as having the second highest grocery expenses in the continental U.S., with residents spending an average of $294.76 weekly. Leading the list is California at $297.72, followed by Nevada, then Mississippi ($290.64), Washington ($287.67), and Florida ($287.27), highlighting the financial challenge faced by Nevada residents in managing their grocery budgets.

For those less inclined towards DIY culinary endeavors, the city's vast selection of dining establishments ensures you'll never dine on ambition alone. The average cost of a three-course meal for two in a mid-range restaurant is around $65, offering a delightful reprieve from the kitchen without breaking the bank.

NAVIGATING THE NEON ROADS: TRANSPORTATION IN LAS VEGAS

It's a city famed for its sprawling boulevard, but Las Vegas is not just a walk on the Strip. For many residents, a car is often more necessity than luxury. The average cost of gasoline hovers around $3.86 per gallon as of early 2024, which is above the national average. Public transportation, though available, is often seen as a secondary option. A monthly pass for the bus system runs about $65, offering a more budget-friendly way to traverse the city's glittering expanse.

THE TAXMAN'S LUCKY DRAW: TAXES IN LAS VEGAS

Las Vegas residents often find themselves with a bit more chip stack in the tax game. Nevada is one of the few states with no personal income tax, making it a jackpot for those used to handing a slice of their earnings to the state. However, this windfall is balanced by higher sales taxes. The sales tax in Las Vegas is currently set at 8.375%, a blend of Nevada's state rate of 4.6% and Clark County's rate of 3.775%. This rate is consistent across Henderson, North Las Vegas, and the rest of Clark County.

When it comes to what's taxed, non-food items generally bear the brunt in Nevada. Most food items bought in grocery stores dodge this tax, though there are exceptions. Treats like candy find themselves taxed, while soda escapes it. Alcoholic beverages, however, aren't so lucky. Services, as a rule, tend to sidestep sales tax in the Silver State. Among the items enjoying a tax-free status are farm equipment and newspapers.

The absence of a state income tax in Nevada is often touted as a major perk of living in the state. This is feasible partly because the state coffers are significantly replenished by tourists, through hotel room taxes and levies on casino revenues, alongside sales and property taxes. In the casino of life, Las Vegas offers a tax structure that's more of a gentle shuffle than a high-stakes deal.

VEGAS LIVING: BETTING ON THE RIGHT SALARY

In the dazzling, ever-twinkling world of Las Vegas, where fortunes can turn on the spin of a roulette wheel, there lies a concept far removed from the glittering casino floors yet fundamentally crucial to the city's heartbeat: the living wage. This isn't about the minimum wage, mind you—the bare minimum legally mandated by those in the halls of power—but rather the true cost of living in this neon oasis, calculated for those striving not just to survive but to live with a semblance of comfort and dignity (and have some fun along the way!).

Now, for a moment, let's park the glitz and glamour and delve into the nuts and bolts of everyday life, where full-time employment isn't a gamble but a necessity, clocking in at 2080 hours a year. It's here, in this bustling desert metropolis, that the MIT Living Wage Calculator casts its analytical eye, offering a glimpse into what it truly takes to make ends meet in Las Vegas.

Why, you might wonder, does the addition of children into this equation cause the required living wage to escalate so dramatically? Well, anyone who's ever tried to pacify a hungry toddler or finance a teenager's seemingly endless needs can attest to the exponential growth of expenses with the arrival of each new family member. From diapers to daycare, school supplies to soccer practice, each child introduces a new set of financial demands, propelling the living wage upward with each additional tiny footstep.

Let's take a closer look at how this plays out, shall we? Following is a table, a sort of financial roadmap, if you will, illustrating the varying living wages necessary to navigate the bustling streets of Las Vegas, depending on one's household composition:

	Number of Children	Living Wage	Poverty Wage
1 ADULT	0 Children	$16.86	$6.53
	1 Child	$35.60	$8.80
	2 Children	$46.41	$11.07
	3 Children	$62.33	$13.34
2 ADULTS (1 WORKING)	0 Children	$27.42	$8.80
	1 Child	$33.78	$11.07
	2 Children	$38.76	$13.34
	3 Children	$44.35	$15.61
2 ADULTS (BOTH WORKING)	0 Children	$13.17	$4.40
	1 Child	$19.90	$5.54
	2 Children	$25.40	$6.67
	3 Children	$31.25	$7.81

Source: MIT Living Wage Calculator, February 2024

EPILOGUE: LIVING IN THE GLOW OF LAS VEGAS

When the curtain falls, Las Vegas occupies a middle tier on the cost-of-living scale among major US cities. Its housing market is a beacon of relative affordability in a country where many urban centers are financially prohibitive. The utility costs are a necessary aspect of desert living, with sustainable options available. Groceries and dining, similarly, offer a spectrum of choices to suit diverse budgets and culinary preferences.

Thus, Las Vegas emerges as a city where the dream of a comfortable life, amidst the allure of endless entertainment and opportunity, is palpably within reach. Its blend of manageable living costs against the backdrop of economic diversity creates a compelling proposition for those seeking a new beginning.

5.   CHOOSING THE RIGHT NEIGHBORHOOD

As a place to live, Las Vegas might appear to exist as a singular entity to the uninitiated. But venture beyond the tourist trails and you'll stumble upon a rich mosaic of neighborhoods, each with its own distinct narrative, vibrancy, and community. This chapter explores Las Vegas's diverse residential realms, in the factors such as affordability, educational prowess, commuting realities, and that ever-intangible "vibe."

Currently, the most sought-after living areas snugly fit within the "C" shape formed by Interstate 215 west to US 15, with Henderson, a city 16 miles southeast of downtown Las Vegas, standing out as a significant exception. This coveted zone encompasses a variety of neighborhoods, offering a home to match almost any taste, lifestyle, or budget. Other areas, especially on the east side, can be more budget-friendly but might not presently provide the same level of safety and appeal.

If you're still unsure where you'll be planting your work roots (or if you're just a glutton for variety), consider setting up camp between the US95-I15 intersection and Decatur Blvd. Residing near this central area is like hitting the real estate jackpot—it gives you the edge in the high-roller game of commuting because you're strategically placed near quick routes to either side of town. Whether your work lands you in the east with Green Valley and Henderson, or you're betting on the west with Summerlin, you've got a winning hand.

Conversely, living across town from your job and commuting is definitely playing against the house in the game of traffic, with a daily takeaway of bumper-to-bumper action. Nevertheless, despite local complaints about traffic, your commute is likely to be much more manageable compared to that in other cities.

DOWNTOWN LAS VEGAS: A SYMPHONY OF VIBRANCY AND REBIRTH

Downtown Las Vegas, often overshadowed by the glittering allure of the Strip, is a vibrant tapestry of community and innovation, a place where the charm of historic Vegas meets the forward pulse of the future. For those considering calling this dynamic enclave home, it offers a living environment rich in contrasts and brimming with possibilities.

At the heart of Downtown's renaissance is a commitment to blending the old with the new. Historic buildings and neon signs stand shoulder-to-shoulder with modern developments, creating a living space that respects its roots while incorporating the promise of the future. The International Innovation Center@Vegas, for instance, symbolizes this shift, serving as a hub for cutting-edge technologies and industries that aim to shape the future of not just Nevada, but potentially the world.

Downtown Las Vegas isn't just about work, however. It's also about the unique experience it offers to its residents. The Fremont Street area provide a daily backdrop of cultural history and entertainment, while the burgeoning Arts District, known as 18b, pulses with creativity, offering art walks, galleries, and a variety of live performances that infuse the area with unique, artistic vibrancy.

Living in Downtown Las Vegas means embracing a lifestyle that's both densely suburban and uniquely urban. The streets here are lined with a mix of high-rise apartments and charming single-family homes, catering to a range of lifestyle preferences and budgets.

The economic vibrancy of Downtown promises stability and growth for its residents with its pro-business environment and opportunities not just in the arts, but emerging technologies and healthcare, as well. The Las Vegas Medical District, with its significant projected economic impact, underscores the neighborhood's role as a center of innovation and health.

Downtown Las Vegas offers its residents a chance to be part of a neighborhood that's evolving, vibrant, and deeply connected to both its past and its future. It's a community where the daily rhythm is a blend of historic charm and modern innovation, where the quality of life is measured not just in amenities but in the rich tapestry of cultural, educational, and economic opportunities available right at your doorstep. For those looking to plant roots in a place that celebrates diversity, creativity, and innovation, Downtown Las Vegas beckons as a compelling choice.

Affordability: Housing spans from hip, modern apartments to charming, older residences, with median listing price for a home swirling around $336K—a veritable beacon for urbanites.

Schools: A breeding ground for creativity and culture, Downtown's educational landscape is still in flux, with opportunities for families to get involved and help shape the evolving school system.

Commute: Residing at the core of Vegas life turns the idea of a dreaded commute into a mere stroll or a quick bike ride amidst the urban tapestry.

Community Vibe: Downtown is a melting pot of innovation that embraces artists, entrepreneurs, and visionaries, marked by the iconic Fremont Street Experience and a burgeoning Arts District.

Cons: The educational landscape is still evolving, which might be a concern for families. The east and the middle part of the neighborhood can be noisy and crowded, not ideal for those seeking tranquility.

ENTERPRISE: THE MODERN FRONTIER

In the sunbaked expanses of the Las Vegas Valley lies a place that seems to defy the usual expectations of desert living—Enterprise. Not to be confused with a certain starship, Enterprise is a thriving and very much earthbound town, a testament to what can happen when suburban planning and a dash of entrepreneurial spirit collide.

Founded on a crisp December day in 1996, Enterprise has blossomed from a patch of Nevada scrub into a buzzing unincorporated town that's as lively as it is diverse. The population rocketed from a modest 14,676 in 2000 to a whopping 221,831 by the 2020 census. This isn't just growth, it's an explosion, propelling Enterprise into the league of "places you might actually want to live" faster than an adventure-bound spacecraft.

So what's the draw, you ask? Well, for starters, it's got the kind of schools that make you wish you were a kid again. And let's not forget the libraries—yes, plural. The Enterprise Library and Windmill Library aren't just places to borrow books, they are community hubs where knowledge meets daily, local life.

Demographically, Enterprise is a mosaic of cultures. It's a melting pot where the median household sings to the tune of $84,298, and the median home hovers around $460,000. It's young, too, with a median age of 35.2 years, making it the kind of place that's as energetic as it is enterprising.

And speaking of enterprising… the local economy is nothing to scoff at, with over 66,000 people employed across sectors like arts, entertainment, recreation, and that Vegas staple, accommodation and food service.

Getting around is a breeze, thanks to a web of highways and state routes that crisscross the landscape, linking Enterprise to the wider world (or at least to the rest of the Las Vegas Valley). The community vibe is decidedly suburban, but peppered with enough bars, restaurants, and thoughtfully-designed parks to keep even the most ardent of city-slickers entertained. It's a place where the neighborhoods aren't just kid-friendly, they're practically kid-paradise, with Mountain's Edge standing out as a particularly coveted spot.

Affordability: With a median home price of around $460,000, Enterprise offers a contemporary living experience that combines modern amenities with the essence of suburban comfort.

Schools: The area is served by a mix of public and private schools, emphasizing a modern education system that prepares students for the future with state-of-the-art facilities and programs.

Commute: Positioned just a short drive from the heart of Las Vegas, Enterprise provides its residents with the convenience of urban living without the traffic jams, making it an attractive location for those who value accessibility.

Community Vibe: Enterprise is vibrant and energetic, marked by its shopping centers, parks, and an array of dining options that cater to the tastes of a diverse population. It's a community that's always bustling, yet retains a warm, welcoming atmosphere.

Cons: Rapid development could lead to issues like traffic congestion, and a more recently developed community can lack the established feel of older neighborhoods.

GREEN VALLEY: THE HARMONIOUS BLEND

Nestled within the sun-drenched expanses of Henderson, Green Valley stands as a testament to the American dream of planned suburban bliss. Conceived by the visionary minds at American Nevada Corporation back in the heady days of 1978, Green Valley proudly holds the title of Southern Nevada's inaugural master-planned community, a precursor to the likes of Summerlin that would follow in its well-considered footsteps.

This community is a veritable oasis of suburban tranquility, meshed seamlessly with the convenience of urban living. Its streets are lined with everything from chic boutiques to welcoming diners, not to mention the recreational facilities that cater to every imaginable pastime, including spirited tennis matches under the desert sky.

Divided into charming enclaves like Green Valley Ranch, Green Valley South, and Green Valley North, the area is inhabited by some 17,298 residents, a cultural blend of 62% Caucasian, 15% Hispanic, and a smattering of other ethnicities. The residents boast an impressive scholarly bent, with a notable 23% clutching Master's degrees or higher—a statistic that comfortably eclipses the national figure. The median household income is an impressive $109,701, dwarfing the national median and painting a picture of comfortable prosperity.

Over in Green Valley North and Green Valley South, the story is much the same, with populations of 44,295 and 27,431, respectively. These areas are also vibrantly diverse. And indeed, the encompassing spirit of Green Valley is one of robust community engagement, where neighbors gather with enthusiasm, warmth, and camaraderie. Green Valley's proximity to the buzz of Henderson and the wider Las Vegas metropolitan area means that residents enjoy the best of both worlds: serene suburban life just a stone's throw from the glitter and excitement of city attractions.

Among residents, the local sentiment is one of deep satisfaction and pride in their community, buoyed by the bounty of amenities, including lush parks and diverse dining options. This feeling is further strengthened by the indomitable community spirit, as seen in their frequent community gatherings and volunteer activities, as well as an emphasis on quality of life, safety, education, and recreational opportunities. In the grand scheme of things, Green Valley represents a slice of Nevada that embodies the essence of community and truly feels like home.

Affordability: Navigating a comfortable middle path, the median home price here makes a gentle landing at $464,000.

Schools: Boasting some of the area's most respected educational institutions, Green Valley stands as a testament to high-caliber learning.

Commute: Its strategic locale ensures swift access to the Strip while maintaining a comforting buffer from the metropolitan hum.

Community Vibe: Green Valley is known for its community gatherings and diverse culinary and shopping destinations, all underscored by an overarching neighborly camaraderie.

Cons: As part of Henderson, it shares the potential for overdevelopment. The area may also lack the vibrant cultural scene found in more urban settings.

HENDERSON: LAS VEGAS'S FAMILY-FRIENDLY FRONTIER

Hidden on the southern fringe of the Las Vegas Valley, Henderson unfolds like a chapter from a sprawling American tale, a city that has swelled from its humble beginnings in 1941 to a bustling community of 331,415 souls as of 2022. This little city, named in a nod to Charles

Henderson, is sprawled across 106.92 square miles, knitting together a story of growth and community under the watchful eyes of Mayor Michelle Romero and the city's council-manager governance.

Now, Henderson isn't just any city. It's a place that prides itself on safety, wearing the title of 35th safest city in the U.S. like a badge of honor. Henderson is also a green haven in the desert. With 71 parks dotting its landscape, the area could well be mistaken for a slice of verdant paradise, an accolade underscored by its over three-decade-long recognition as a Tree City USA.

These parks aren't just patches of grass and playground equipment; they're inclusive realms offering everything from serene walking paths to lively sports areas, not to mention dog parks and programs for all abilities. It's no wonder the city's parks and rec system is nationally accredited—five times over, no less.

Nestled within a blend of urban development and community vibrancy, Henderson presents two distinct faces: the evolving, modern West Henderson and the traditional, less polished East Henderson, sometimes cheekily nicknamed "Hendertucky." This nickname, particularly aimed at East Henderson, draws a humorous yet critical comparison to stereotypes associated with rural Kentucky, reflecting on its older neighborhoods and a more contentious social atmosphere—a stark contrast to the glossy allure of Las Vegas.

While "Hendertucky" might underscore the tight knit, albeit controversial aspects of East Henderson's character, West Henderson tells a different story. It epitomizes the suburban dream with its newer developments, safer neighborhoods, and proximity to city amenities, offering a clear delineation within the same city. This contrast not only highlights the diverse community dynamics but also the ongoing evolution from the cozy, neighborly vibe of "old"

Henderson to the more desirable and modern lifestyle found in its western expanses.

Economically, Henderson is as robust as they come, with a median household income that'll make you whistle ($85,311) and a business landscape thriving with over 5,500 employer firms as of 2017. And when residents aren't busy contributing to the city's $5 billion retail sales, they're likely enjoying a commute that's under 24 minutes, on average.

The city offers places of worship for numerous denominations, as well as golf courses greener than you'd expect in a desert, thanks to some clever use of raw and reclaimed water. Henderson's slogan, "A Place to Call Home," isn't just a catchy phrase; it's a promise, a declaration of the city's spirit of community and belonging, punctuated by a calendar bursting with events that draw families closer under the vast Nevada sky.

Affordability: The median home price stands at $455,000, providing a golden mean of value and quality living.

Schools: Its schools rank well, with dedicated educators and vibrant programs steering the young minds of tomorrow.

Commute: Roughly 16 miles from the Strip, Henderson strikes a balance between proximity to economic hubs and the tranquility of suburban life.

Community Vibe: Henderson thrives on its community ethos, characterized by well-tended parks, a vibrant local culture, and a palpable commitment to public safety.

Cons: Could be too quiet for those seeking urban excitement. On the other hand, the area has been experiencing rapid growth, which might lead to congestion and overdevelopment concerns.

HISTORIC WESTSIDE: THE SOUL OF LAS VEGAS

Nested in the bustling heart of Las Vegas, the Historic Westside neighborhood is a living, breathing history lesson, brimming with the echoes of a bygone era and the palpable buzz of a future so bright, you'd need sunglasses to contemplate it. This little corner of the world is a veritable smorgasbord of stories and savory delights, ready to tickle the fancy of anyone pondering a change of scenery to this vibrant enclave.

Our tale unfurls in the late 1940s, amidst a backdrop where the glittering allure of the Strip summoned Black entertainers with its siren song, only to give them the cold shoulder when the curtain fell. It was the Historic Westside, with Jackson Avenue at its heart, that rolled out the welcome mat, offering a nocturnal sanctuary within its quartet of Black-owned clubs—a haven of solace and festivity. As the pages of the 1950s turned, the area stood witness to a groundbreaking leap towards integration, heralded by the Moulin Rouge Hotel. This shining beacon of unity, the first of its ilk across the nation, now lives on in the hallowed halls of the Neon Museum as a proud testament to the neighborhood's rich tapestry.

Today, the Historic Westside is undergoing a transformation, led by a vibrant and tantalizing culinary scene. At the helm of this delicious revolution are establishments like the West Side Oasis bar and restaurant, the latest jewel in the neighborhood's crown; and Gritz Cafe, where Trina Jiles—a trailblazer in both the firefighting and culinary arenas—weaves her magic. Fueling this gastronomic uprising is the UNLV Tourism Business Igniter, armed with a $2.1 million federal grant, poised to catapult local hospitality and tourism ventures to new heights with an arsenal of support services.

The area's transformational narrative is exemplified by the Historic Westside School, built as a two-room schoolhouse in 1923 and now a $12.5 million center of community engagement following a seven-year facelift. This architectural phoenix now hosts an abundance of meetings, lectures, trainings, and all types of events related to community engagement. Driving this resurgence is the HUNDRED Plan, a community-concocted elixir for future prosperity, blessed by the Las Vegas City Council. This visionary blueprint is gently nudging the Historic Westside towards what one hopes will be a renaissance of dazzling proportions.

Safety, that ever-present concern, has seen local law enforcement and community stalwarts link arms in a spirited bid to weave a tighter safety net in the face of ongoing challenges. This united front is steadfastly crafting a safer, more serene haven for its denizens.

Affordability: The Historic Westside area offers some of the most accessible housing in the city, with median home prices around $328,000—a great fit for those seeking both affordability and historical significance.

Schools: Education in the Historic Westside is deeply rooted in community values, with schools that are revitalizing their programs to provide students with both a rich understanding of their heritage and the tools for success—curriculums that continue with the area's commitment to recognizing the past while looking towards a bright future.

Commute: Its proximity to downtown Las Vegas ensures that residents are never far from the city's amenities, with a streamlined commute that allows for immersion in the neighborhood's vibrant street life.

Community Vibe: The Historic Westside is a close-knit community, where festivals, music, and local eateries celebrate the cultural legacy of the area. It's a place where history is alive and every street tells a story.

Cons: The area has faced social and economic challenges, but gentrification and redevelopment continue to reshape the neighborhood's profile.

NORTH LAS VEGAS: A CITY WITHIN A CITY

In the less-glittery shadow of its brightly-lit neighbor, the story of North Las Vegas continues to unfold—a narrative far removed from the bustling casinos and crowded streets that first come to mind. In this slice of Nevada, the community thrives on the kind of grit and gumption that powers industries and propels cities into the future. It's a place where the hum of machinery and the promise of tomorrow's jobs fill the air, with an astounding 17.7 million square feet of industrial space stretching its steel bones skyward, ready to bolster the local economy and redefine the urban landscape.

Nestled amidst this industrial ballet, significant projects emerge, like the sprawling 11-million-square-foot endeavor by Prologis at Apex Industrial Park, an 18,000-acre testament to ambition with 7,000 acres ripe for innovation. The city, with its forward-thinking investment of over $63 million in vital infrastructure, is setting the stage for a booming and bustling future.

The Helios Medical Campus and the Vegas Industrial Park, formerly known as the Speedway Industrial Park, are the crown jewels in North Las Vegas's ambitious development plan. These projects are not just about buildings and land—they're about breathing new life into the community, creating jobs, and offering residents health, success, and prosperity.

But North Las Vegas is more than its economic ventures. It's a city with a vibrant heart, home to approximately 280,543 souls as of mid-2022, marking an impressive 8.1% population surge since 2020. The streets buzz with the energy of a youthful demographic, demonstrating that the city is a place of growth in more ways than one.

Diversity paints the very fabric of this community, with a rich tapestry of cultures living side by side. Economically, it's a city on the rise, with a median household income of $71,774, supported by a backbone of industries that range from hospitality to health care.

The city's landscape is dotted with parks and trails, offering spaces for recreation and reflection, and housing developments are on the rise, working towards a future where everyone can find a place to call home.

Affordability: Housing in North Las Vegas is generally more affordable than in some other parts of the Las Vegas Valley, offering a variety of options for first-time homebuyers and families looking for value. The median home price stands at $404,000,

Schools: The area is home to numerous public schools, with efforts underway to improve educational facilities and opportunities for its growing population.

Commute: Located on the northern edge of the Las Vegas Valley, it provides residents with access to major highways and thoroughfares, making commutes to other parts of the city manageable.

Community Vibe: North Las Vegas emphasizes the importance of community, with numerous parks, recreational facilities, and public centers that serve as gathering places for residents of all ages.

Cons: Historically, it has faced economic challenges and infrastructure issues. The area might not offer the same level of amenities as more affluent neighborhoods.

NORTHWEST: A HIDDEN GEM AMIDST THE BUSTLE

Northwest Las Vegas offers a tranquil retreat with the charm of suburban life, coupled with the convenience of city living. Here lies a splendid fusion of small-town charm and urban practicality, a place where growth is a tangible reality, not just a buzzword. The area's close connection to Mt. Charleston brings a unique blend of natural beauty and outdoor adventure to the community's doorstep, offering residents and visitors alike an easy escape to the great outdoors, hiking trails, and scenic vistas.

The roads have stretched and widened, and a diverse array of businesses continue to materialize. Take, for instance, Casa Real Mexican Restaurant—located in the food-centric retail center Craig Marketplace—where the flavors of Mexico dance on the tongue, or the family-owned G.O.A.T Pickleball, an all-encompassing, one-stop shop for enthusiasts of the hugely popular sport.

When it comes to setting down roots, Northwest Las Vegas presents a compelling argument for those looking to attain extra square footage and backyard expanses without breaking the bank, offering more real estate bang-for-your-buck compared to some of its suburban cousins.

And then there's the call of the wild—parks, trails, and desert vistas that beckon the adventurous spirit. It's this proximity to nature's doorstep that adds a unique flavor to Northwest Las Vegas, marrying the convenience of city living with the serenity of the great outdoors.

Community spirit here is more than just a notion, it's a tangible part of everyday life. Local events, farmers' markets, and places to gather knit the residents together, creating strong and long-lasting community ties.

Affordability: The Northwest is a haven for those seeking value, with median home prices hovering around $437,000. It represents a blend of affordability and quality living in the Las Vegas area.

Schools: This area is known for its commitment to education, hosting a variety of schools that cater to fostering the growth and development of young minds in a supportive environment.

Commute: Its strategic location ensures a relatively easy commute to downtown Las Vegas, making it an ideal spot for professionals and families alike who desire a quiet home life within reach of the city's pulse.

Community Vibe: The Northwest is characterized by its friendly neighborhoods, outdoor parks, and community events that bring residents together, creating a strong sense of belonging and community spirit.

Cons: Northwest Las Vegas can feel isolated from the main city's attractions; the area has limited dining and shopping options compared to more central neighborhoods.

PARADISE: THE URBAN MELTING POT

The modestly-named Paradise, Nevada is nestled right next to the Neon City itself, and embodies its location by offering the perfect blend of everyday life mixed with the glittery existence of the Strip. This spot is famed for rolling out the red carpet to the iconic "Welcome to Fabulous Las Vegas" sign and playing host to the scholarly pursuits of the University of Nevada, Las Vegas (UNLV). But Paradise is not defined solely by its proximity to Las Vegas—the unincorporated town in Clark County is a unique and robust place to live in its own right, since 1950, that continues to demonstrate its singularity by dodging Las Vegas's taxman.

Now, if we're talking numbers—and I do find them rather compelling in a nerdy sort of way—Paradise boasts a hearty population of 191,238 souls, according to the 2020 census. It stands as one of the United States' most populated spots that doesn't *quite* make it to city status. Its diverse locals are from an array of ethnic backgrounds, and this mélange of cultures brings a zest to the local lifestyle, flavors the cuisine, and infuses its gatherings and events with an undeniable exuberance.

Paradise isn't just a backdrop to the high-rolling antics of the Las Vegas Strip economically, either; it's a heavyweight on its own, especially in the realms of tourism and entertainment. The area's accommodations and eateries raked in a cool $19 billion in 2017. But it's not all about showbiz; the workforce here is refreshingly varied, with involvement in industries such as healthcare, social assistance, and transportation.

But wait, there's more! True to its name, Paradise offers a slice of the American dream, with a variety of housing options and a average home value of $355,000. Here, families, professionals, and students come together to create a dynamic community.

Affordability: Housing options range from upscale apartments to more budget-friendly homes, with an average price around $355,000.

Schools: The neighborhood houses several educational institutions, offering a variety of proficiency levels—although currently, some schools perform below state averages.

Commute: Residing here means being at the heart of Vegas, greatly reducing commute times.

Community Vibe: Renowned for its dynamic nightlife and cultural richness, Paradise is ideal for those looking for a lively, cosmopolitan lifestyle.

Cons: The proximity to the Strip can mean more noise and traffic, and the area might feel too commercialized for those seeking a traditional residential environment.

SPRING VALLEY: THE COZY SUBURBAN HAVEN

Nestled within the expansive embrace of the Las Vegas Valley, Spring Valley stands as a testament to thoughtful community planning and the fulfilling lifestyle that can be found in the Nevada desert. From its inception in the mid-1970s, when Pardee Homes transformed the remnants of the Stardust International Raceway into a master-planned community, Spring Valley has grown both in size and in spirit. Today, it sprawls over 33 square miles, housing a diverse community of over 215,597 souls, according to the latest census.

This neighborhood, while offering the serene suburban life, keeps the electrifying energy of Las Vegas within arm's reach. It's a place where you won't find towering casinos or sprawling hotels, but instead discover a vibrant modern Chinatown that emerged in 1995, thanks to the foresight of the Taiwanese American JHK Investment Group. This district alone has become a cultural hub, attracting visitors and residents alike with its ethnic Chinese and other pan-Asian businesses including popular restaurants that serve up sumptuous, authentic cuisine. At the core of the district is Chinatown Plaza, with its ornate, Tang Dynasty-style entryway, where you can attend events and find numerous shops, restaurants, and even a Chinese martial arts school.

Spring Valley's residential fabric is woven with single-family homes, townhomes, and condominiums, accommodating a wide array of lifestyles and preferences. The community's median household income of $63,494 speaks to the comfortable living standards here, supported by a robust local economy that employs around 112,000 people.

Education is a cornerstone of the community. Spring Valley High School, for example, serves 2,573 students and boasts an impressive 92% graduation rate, reflecting the community's commitment to nurturing the next generation.

Affordability: It is a real estate haven with diverse housing options; the median home price of around $398,000 caters to a wide range of budgets.

Schools: The area boasts a mix of respected public and private schools, catering to families seeking a robust educational environment.

Commute: Located just a short drive from the city's heart, it offers a balance of easy access and quiet living.

Community Vibe: Spring Valley is celebrated for its cultural diversity and community-focused amenities, making it an ideal spot for families and young professionals alike.

Cons: The area is experiencing growth-related issues like traffic and overcrowding in schools. In addition, the nightlife and cultural amenities can feel limited compared to Downtown.

SUMMERLIN: THE PINNACLE OF SUBURBIA

Perched on the western edge of the Las Vegas Valley and named after the grandmother of billionaire Howard Hughes, Summerlin offers breathtaking views of the Spring Mountain Range and Red Rock Canyon. This master-planned community has neatly divided North, South, and West associations, and is a meticulously designed, affluent neighborhood with high standards for quality of life.

Within the bounds of Summerlin, 22 distinct villages—each with its own flair and architectural theme—create a living patchwork quilt of personal styles and amenities. The air seems fresher, the parks greener, and the lifestyle more abundant than anywhere else.

The population, a hearty mix of about 137,330 residents, ranges from eager young professionals to contented retirees, all drawn here by the allure of above-average public schools and a welcoming, family-oriented atmosphere. There are more than 250 parks, a trail system that stretches over 150 miles, and no fewer than 10 golf courses—a veritable playground for the active and the leisurely alike.

Downtown Summerlin serves as the heart of the community, featuring more than 125 shops, bars, and eateries, including a Regal Cinemas movie theater. Sports enthusiasts have their pick of venues, from the City National Arena (home base for the Vegas Golden Knights) to the Las Vegas Ballpark (the stadium that the Las Vegas Aviators will call their home field).

Summerlin's accolades are many—from being named Community of the Year to features in *National Geographic*, the area has been lauded for its design and planning. Managed by three master associations and patrolled by the dedicated officers of the Las Vegas Metropolitan Police Department Summerlin Area Command, it's also a community that feels safe and sound to its residents.

Now, onto the topic of habitation. The real estate market here is as lively as a Las Vegas show, with the median sale price of homes swirling around the $602,000 mark, evidence of the community's desirability and the steady appreciation of property values. Yet, as with any market, fluctuations are part of the dance, with prices dipping, diving, and doing an occasional jitterbug.

Affordability: Aim for the stars, and you'll find Summerlin, where the median home price orbits around $602,000, marking it as a premium residential enclave.

Schools: Education shines bright here, with several schools garnering accolades and top rankings statewide, making it a magnet for families.

Commute: A mere 20 minutes from the Strip's dazzle (given the traffic on any given day, of course), this serene suburb offers a daily retreat from urban frenzy.

Community Vibe: Picture weekend farmers' markets, jogging trails winding through verdant expanses, and a convivial atmosphere where neighbors know each other by name.

Cons: High cost of living may be prohibitive for some, and the area is quite homogeneous, which might not appeal to those seeking a more diverse community.

SUNRISE: THE EASTERN OASIS

Nestled just a hop, skip, and a jump away from Las Vegas lies the Sunrise neighborhood, a little slice of Americana perched on the western base of Frenchman Mountain. It's part of the sprawling expanse of unincorporated town Sunrise Manor, which is home to a population of 205,618 souls according to the 2020 census. In fact, it would be considered one of the biggest cities in Nevada it was incorporated. This isn't just a place where people live; it's where they come together, sharing in the joys and challenges of daily life. The significant Latino presence signals not just diversity in the city's cultural identity, but in daily life as a resident too, with Mexican restaurants, grocery stores, and the sounds of mariachi bands playing on summer weekends.

When it comes to understanding the safety of the Sunrise neighborhood, the local community paints a complex picture. Some note areas around Sunrise Hospital as rundown and sketchy, with a visible homeless component. However, others are more positive, describing Sunrise as generally safe, with a strong community feel, friendly neighbors, and a family-friendly atmosphere. In summary, while there are areas of concern (as is frequently the case with big cities), the overall sentiment towards Sunrise suggests a place where safety and neighborliness prevail.

Affordability: With median home prices around $314,000, Sunrise is an attractive option for those seeking a balance between affordability and the allure of desert living.

Schools: The area is home to several schools that pride themselves on creating nurturing environments for students, with a focus on community engagement and academic excellence.

Commute: Located just a short distance from the city center, Sunrise residents enjoy a straightforward commute that allows them to access the broader Las Vegas area and easily return to the tranquility of their neighborhood.

Community Vibe: Sunrise is characterized by its quiet streets, community parks, and a laid-back lifestyle that encourages outdoor activities and neighborhood gatherings, making it a perfect setting for those who enjoy a slower pace of life.

Cons: Limited access to high-end amenities, and some areas might lack the development seen in more affluent neighborhoods.

THE LAKES: A DESERT MIRAGE TURNED REALITY

Tucked away within the city limits of Las Vegas, Nevada, lies a little oasis known as The Lakes, an affluent master-planned community that could easily be mistaken for a slice of waterfront heaven rather than a desert enclave. The neighborhood is two square miles, snug against the backdrop of the Spring Mountains and the scenic vistas of Red Rock Canyon, and offers a living experience that feels more akin to a year-round vacation than the typical suburban sprawl.

Conceived in the halcyon days of the mid-1980s to mid-1990s, The Lakes pioneered the concept of master-planned living in Las Vegas. It was a bold vision of landscaped greenery, communal lakes, and a blend of residential bliss that set the stage for what many in Vegas now aspire to. The centerpiece of this verdant dream is Lake Sahara, a man-made marvel that gives residents the rare privilege of private waterfront living in the heart of the desert.

Here, life moves at a leisurely pace. Residents can choose from a spectrum of homes, ranging from cozy condos to sprawling lakefront estates, all while enjoying the kind of amenities that would make a holiday resort jealous. Imagine starting your day with a jog along tree-lined trails, pausing only to admire the serene beauty of Lake Sahara, or perhaps winding down with a leisurely boat ride at sunset, fishing rod in hand, as the Las Vegas skyline twinkles in the distance.

The Lakes, with its vast collection of over 5,000 homes, offers an array of real estate options, from lavish lakeside living to introductory starter homes and sophisticated condos. The housing market is healthy, reflecting the desirability of the area, with the median sales price for homes indicating a premium on lakeside luxury.

Safety and education are paramount in The Lakes, with low crime rates and access to variety of schools, making it ideal for families. And while it may sit just east of Summerlin, The Lakes holds its own, offering a blend of seclusion and convenience that's hard to find. With shopping, dining, and entertainment just moments away, residents enjoy the best of both worlds: the tranquility of lakeside living with the vibrancy of Las Vegas at their doorstep.

Affordability: This neighborhood balances lakeside serenity and the convenience of urban proximity for a price that reflects its desirability, with median home prices perching at around $640,000,

Schools: The local education facilities serve the community well, nurturing a well-rounded, next-generation.

Commute: Just a stone's throw—or, more accurately, a 20-minute drive—from the Strip, so you can get back to tranquil waters after enjoying the buzz of the Neon City.

Community Vibe: Here, life is an outdoor affair, where weekends mean boat rides, fishing, or leisurely promenades along the water.

Cons: Limited in terms of cultural amenities and dining options, and the artificial lakes require significant maintenance and ecological considerations.

WHITNEY: A CONTRASTINGLY SUBURBAN

Nestled in the shadow of the more serene landscapes of Paradise and Henderson, , lies the quaint suburb of Whitney. I must admit that I've never actually heard anyone refer to it as the Whitney area. In my mind, it's always just been part of Henderson's outskirts. But then again, who am I to dispute the wisdom of the Clark County's administrators?

Once known to the world as East Las Vegas, Whitney has since shrugged off its city moniker in favor of a more subdued identity, one that speaks to its 49,061 souls seeking their own slice of the American dream, Vegas-style.

However, Whitney is not all quiet streets and community spirit. The undercurrents of safety concerns ripple through the neighborhood. Polls reveal a significant portion of the community on edge. The crime statistics highlight the need for increased crime prevention and safety measures—but some pockets of Whitney shine brighter, offering safer havens and a reminder of the community's resilience.

Whitney is no stranger to hardship. The ripple effects of a faltering tourism sector during the pandemic have left their mark, with the specter of poverty casting a long shadow over nearly a fifth of its households. The dreams of higher education and prosperity remain just out of reach for many, with a stark number of adult residents having never donned a graduation cap.

Whitney, then, is a study in contrasts: a suburban setting where nature's beauty is a backdrop to daily life, a community that faces economic challenges with a steadfast spirit, and a neighborhood navigating the complexities of safety in the shadow of Sin City. It's a place where the suburban dream is still within reach, but currently requires a side of vigilance. For those considering a move, Whitney offers the promise of a quieter life, with both the splendor and the challenges that come with being a stone's throw from Las Vegas.

Affordability: The median home price in Whitney stands at an inviting $340,000, presenting an appealing option for families and individuals seeking quality living without the hefty price tag.

Schools: Whitney's schools are the heart of the community, offering a range of educational programs that cater to the diverse needs of its students. The focus here is on creating a supportive and enriching learning environment that encourages academic and personal growth.

Commute: Its location offers residents easy access to the main thoroughfares leading into Las Vegas, ensuring that the commute to work or entertainment is convenient—and yet maintains a serene atmosphere, untouched by the city's frenzy.

Community Vibe: Whitney is celebrated for its parks and recreational areas, fostering an active and engaged community. Here, weekends are spent at local sports fields, community centers, or simply enjoying the great outdoors. It's an ideal place for those looking to settle down in a calm and welcoming environment.

Cons: Further from the Las Vegas core, which could impact commute times and access to city amenities. Development is less dense, which might not appeal to all.

EPILOGUE: SELECTING YOUR SLICE OF LAS VEGAS

Embarking on a residential voyage through Las Vegas's neighborhoods reveals the multifaceted nature of this desert jewel. Whether you're drawn to the choreographed beauty of Summerlin, the warm embrace of Henderson, the dynamic pulse of Downtown, the serene waterfront vistas of The Lakes, or Green Valley's balanced allure, Las Vegas extends an invitation to discover a home that resonates with your aspirations and lifestyle preferences.

As you chart your course, remember that Las Vegas isn't just an entertainer on the world stage—it's a mosaic of communities, teeming with opportunities, each waiting to offer its warmest welcome. The city, with its myriad neighborhoods, stands as a bastion of diversity, promising a place for every dream under its vast, starlit sky.

6.   REAL ESTATE ESSENTIALS

Las Vegas may be a global hub of entertainment, gambling, and—let's be honest, a few impulsive, questionable decisions—but it's also a place people call home. In this chapter, we'll untangle the often bewildering world of the Las Vegas residential real estate market. We'll compare the heartfelt joy of home ownership with the free-spirited nature of renting and explore the architectural options, from single-family homes to garden-style and mid-rise apartments, along with some stats and numbers along the way.

RENTING VS. BUYING: THE GREAT DEBATE

In one corner, we have buying—like planting your flag in the parched Nevada soil, declaring, "This is mine!" In the other, renting—a sort of modern nomadic existence, but with better amenities and less moving of livestock.

Buying: In the game of home buying, Las Vegas is dealing a strong hand. As of early 2024, the median home sale price is around $418,000—a figure that might make you blink twice. But if you're venturing into the plush suburbs of Summerlin or Henderson, be prepared for the prices to soar like the fountains at the Bellagio.

A starter home in Vegas—think two bedrooms, one bath, and about 800 square feet of living space—can be had for about $283,000. It's a modest bet in the Vegas property market. For those looking to move up the property ladder, a three bedroom, two bath home, offering a spacious 1,800 square feet, goes for around $394,000. And for the high rollers, luxury homes—those with five or more bedrooms and three or more baths, sprawling over 3,000 square feet—start from $660,000 and climb upwards.

It's a hot market, with nearly 40,000 residences changing hands annually. Popular listings under $400,000 spark bidding wars reminiscent of a high-stakes auction. To stand out in this competitive market, come armed with pre-approval letters and the flexibility and willingness to deal with inspection issues. Real estate in general, and in Las Vegas in particular, is like playing poker—you need to know when to hold 'em and when to fold 'em.

Pros:

- Investment in the Future: Buying a home is not just acquiring living space; it's investing in a tangible asset that, more often than not, appreciates over time. Given Las Vegas' growth, that dusty plot you plant your flag on might just sprout a profit.

- Stability and Freedom: Owning your home means saying goodbye to rent hikes and the whims of landlords. Want to paint your living room flamingo pink? Go right ahead; it's your castle.

- Community Ties: Homeownership tends to anchor you more firmly within a community, fostering deeper connections with neighbors and local engagement.

Cons:

- Upfront Costs: The entry fee to the homeownership club is steep, requiring down payments, closing costs, and possibly a somewhat bruised financial spirit.

- Maintenance and Upkeep: Every leaky faucet, every rebellious HVAC system, becomes your responsibility. Your wallet and weekend plans will need to adjust accordingly.

- Market Risks: While real estate tends to appreciate, it's not immune to fluctuations. The roulette real estate market forces doesn't always land on your number.

Renting: Renting in Las Vegas, on the other hand, offers an appealing flexibility. With median rents floating around $1,362 for a one-bedroom apartment, renting allows for mobility, minimal maintenance worries, and the freedom to flee should your upstairs neighbor decide to set up a home bowling alley. For a smidge more on the price tag, you can upgrade your abode to a swanky modern apartment, complete with the kind of luxury amenities—fitness center, pool, outdoor recreational spaces for activities like picnicking and barbecuing—that will make you feel like a high roller on a daily basis.

Pros:

- Flexibility and Mobility: Not ready to commit to being a Las Vegas lifer? Renting allows you the liberty to move with the ebb and flow of life's changes, job opportunities, or simply the itch for a new view.

- Maintenance is Not Your Problem: Broken air conditioner? Bug problem? Simply call the landlord. Renters are largely freed from the burdens of home repair and maintenance.

- Financial Predictability: Rent, utilities (sometimes), and that's it—no unexpected home repair costs sabotaging your budget.

- Ease of Entry: One of renting's unsung virtues lies in its accessibility. Foregoing the daunting down payment required for home purchases, renting pretty much just needs a security deposit, proof of a stable job, and a decent credit history.

Cons:

- Transient Ties: Rentals can make communities more fluid, potentially making it harder to form lasting neighborhood bonds.

- The Money Pit: Rent checks don't build your equity; they build your landlord's equity. It can feel like an endless cycle of expenditure with no tangible asset to show for it.

- Rules and Restrictions: Ever dreamt of that flamingo-pink living room? Landlord-imposed decor restrictions and the rigidity of rental agreements can bury that dream in the sand.

TO RENT OR TO BUY, THAT IS THE QUESTION

The choice between renting and buying in Las Vegas, much like choosing between the blackjack table and the roulette wheel, is largely one of personal circumstances, risk tolerance, and perhaps a touch of existential pondering.

To buy is to invest in a slice of this ever-evolving city, to bet on its future both as a metropolis and as your home. It's to accept the mantle of homeowner, with all the responsibilities and rewards it entails.

To rent is to embrace flexibility amid uncertainty, to sample the varied flavors of Las Vegas living without the long-term commitment, and perhaps, to keep your options open should life present you with new adventures.

THE STATS THAT TELL THE STORY

Numbers in real estate, much like the caloric content displayed next to food in restaurant menus, can be both enlightening and disheartening. In Las Vegas, the narrative is one of growth, challenge, and opportunity. With the median listing price per square foot standing at around $250, the value proposition of both buying and renting in Las Vegas offers a narrative far removed from the simpler days of its founding.

In the bustling heart of Las Vegas, to acquire a slice of the residential dream, the wheels of fortune and finance must turn in your favor to the tune of earning at least $114,689.16 a year. This is not a figure plucked from the high-rolling tables but one that is firmly grounded in the reality of the median-priced homestead and interest rates. To comfortably shoulder the burdens of principal, interest, taxes, and insurance, this sum is your ticket to homeownership in the city that thrives in the desert's embrace. It ranks as the 20th highest requirement for a metro in the grand tapestry of these United States, a testament to the allure and the cost of calling Las Vegas your home. So, if your salary isn't giving you a Scrooge McDuck moment and lady luck hasn't graced you with a jackpot win, welcome to the world of renting.

Metro Area	Median Home Price	Monthly Payment (PITI)	Salary Needed
San Jose	$1,850,000	$10,913.09	$467,703.99
San Francisco	$1,300,000	$7,855.39	$336,659.66
San Diego	$978,500	$5,723.87	$245,308.63

Los Angeles	$897,600	$5,302.54	$227,251.89
Boston	$745,100	$4,627.01	$198,300.50
Seattle	$744,300	$4,466.15	$191,406.56
New York City	$665,000	$4,412.63	$189,112.70
Denver	$673,000	$3,941.96	$168,941.33
Washington, D.C.	$612,600	$3,754.94	$160,926.04
Miami	$602,500	$3,651.05	$156,473.60
Portland	$593,400	$3,571.00	$153,043.04
Riverside	$565,000	$3,398.57	$145,653.00
Sacramento	$542,000	$3,331.33	$142,771.12
Austin	$485,700	$3,272.88	$140,266.27
Salt Lake City	$554,500	$3,220.96	$138,041.09
Providence	$480,100	$3,110.12	$133,290.87
Raleigh	$478,600	$2,849.69	$122,129.48
Phoenix	$467,200	$2,710.60	$116,168.59
Orlando	$436,500	$2,697.46	$115,605.36
Las Vegas	$460,600	$2,676.08	$114,689.16

Hartford	$375,100	$2,628.01	$112,628.91
Dallas	$385,700	$2,619.07	$112,245.86
National	$406,900	$2,594.11	$111,176.20
Baltimore	$406,300	$2,568.90	$110,095.93
Tampa	$415,000	$2,559.40	$109,688.45
Chicago	$365,100	$2,524.23	$108,181.51
Minneapolis	$387,900	$2,477.83	$106,192.58
Milwaukee	$386,100	$2,464.46	$105,619.62
Nashville	$413,600	$2,462.75	$105,546.39
Philadelphia	$368,500	$2,434.24	$104,324.48
Jacksonville	$390,000	$2,433.05	$104,273.53
Charlotte	$406,900	$2,423.94	$103,883.35
Richmond	$401,700	$2,412.91	$103,410.27
Houston	$345,600	$2,359.78	$101,133.37
Atlanta	$379,200	$2,343.75	$100,446.48
San Antonio	$332,200	$2,247.25	$96,310.85
Virginia Beach	$344,500	$2,132.07	$91,374.30

Columbus	$323,400	$2,085.98	$89,399.00
Kansas City	$328,800	$2,082.42	$89,246.45
Indianapolis	$316,400	$1,917.07	$82,160.11
Birmingham	$310,200	$1,862.94	$79,840.15
Cincinnati	$293,300	$1,856.87	$79,580.33
Buffalo	$260,600	$1,839.96	$78,855.48
New Orleans	$281,500	$1,790.23	$76,724.26
St Louis	$268,600	$1,758.80	$75,376.97
Detroit	$266,600	$1,756.94	$75,297.49
Memphis	$280,000	$1,746.30	$74,841.44
Louisville	$271,900	$1,690.01	$72,429.19
Oklahoma City	$251,200	$1,662.31	$71,241.93
Cleveland	$236,700	$1,606.99	$68,871.06
Pittsburgh	$200,000	$1,370.87	$58,751.54

Source: hsh.com, February 2024

In the quirky world of Las Vegas, the multifamily rental market has been doing a bit of a dance lately, a sort of financial cha-cha with numbers that almost seem to have a mind of their own. Picture this: as of autumn 2023, apartment rents did a little shimmy downwards by 0.3%, bringing the average to a modest $1,490 per month. That's a year-over-year dip of 1.5%, not exactly the sort of drop that makes headlines, but noteworthy nonetheless.

Zillow, always one for keeping an eye on such things, observed a tiny wobble in rental rates too. A two-bedroom abode in the valley, as per their tally, now sits at about $1,808. That's a 0.2 percent toe-tap down from August and a 1.4 percent glide downwards year over year. The Nevada State Apartment Association, with their eagle eyes, noted local rents falling by 2.2 percent in the first quarter of 2023, landing at an average of $1,430 a month. One can almost hear the croupiers shouting, "Place your bets!"

Then there's Zumper, chiming in with data as fresh as February 2024, stating the median rent for all sorts of living spaces in Vegas as $1,800. That's 7% shy of the national average—a small victory, perhaps, in the grand scheme of things. And not to be outdone, Apartment List ranks Vegas as the 52nd most expensive large city in the U.S., with a median rent of $1,395.

Now, let's talk about vacancy rates. They've been fluttering around like loose dollar bills in the desert breeze, but are now nudging closer to what folks call historical norms. After dipping in the second quarter, they slipped an extra 10 basis points to 6.4%. Earlier in 2023, though, they were lounging at a lofty 9.6%, well above the comfy chair of the 7.8% historical average. Avison Young, keeping score, recorded a jump in vacancy rates to 9.0% at the end of Q1 2023.

Rental trends have their own tale to tell. In the more well-heeled neighborhoods, rates have been on a gentle decline, while in the less flashy parts of town like North Las Vegas, they're either stuck in place or inching up. Despite a record-breaking rush of new apartments flooding the market, this expected push-and-pull between vacancy and rental rates hasn't quite played out in full yet.

The Vegas multifamily market has welcomed a 5.5% increase in new inventory but also a 2% dip in average rent.

As for what's stirring the pot in the rental market, a few chefs are at work. New construction is zipping along, with about 1,300 units popping up in the third quarter, adding to the nearly 3,700 units already served up this year. Economic conditions, including job growth and rising wages, are giving the multifamily industry a bit of a boost. Migration patterns, particularly from California and other states, have been adding their flavor, though they've simmered down over the past couple of years. Water concerns—always a hot, dry topic in the desert—are also in the mix. And of course, the classic supply and demand: currently, supply is outpacing demand, leading to more vacancies and rents taking a slight tumble.

For potential renters, this Las Vegas market is like a buffet with more options than you can sample in one visit. With rents on the decline and vacancy rates higher than usual, there's room for some price haggling. The surge in new apartments means choices galore in terms of location, amenities, and styles. However, it's wise to remember that this market, much like the city itself, has its share of unpredictability, so keeping an eye on potential rent fluctuations is prudent.

In a nutshell, Las Vegas's multifamily rental scene is adjusting its bow tie and smoothing out its evening gown, with rents taking a polite step back and vacancy rates stepping up their game. For those looking to snag a rental, this might just be your lucky roll of the dice, but as with any gamble in this dazzling desert city, it's wise to play with a full deck of caution and awareness.

SINGLE-FAMILY HOMES: THE DESERT CASTLES

The single-family home, the cornerstone of the American Dream, sits proudly in Las Vegas neighborhoods like armor-clad knights lounging comfortably in their kingdoms. These homes, ranging from cozy two-bedrooms to sprawling mansions, offer a space truly your own, where the only drumbeat to which you march is the one blaring from your own Bluetooth speaker.

GARDEN-STYLE APARTMENTS: A TOUCH OF GREEN IN THE DESERT

Garden-style apartments, rarely more than a few stories tall and often arranged around courtyards or, indeed, gardens, offer a communal form of living with a nod to the nature that's so often bulldozed to make way for progress. They promise the amenities of apartment life—maintenance staff on call, communal pools, possibly a fitness center—tempered with a layout that somehow feels less towering, less anonymous.

MID-RISE APARTMENTS: REACHING FOR THE SKY, RESPONSIBLY

Mid-rise apartments, standing taller than their garden-style cousins but not quite scraping the sky, offer a blend of density and domesticity. These structures, often found in urban or developing suburban areas, provide a taste of apartment living with fewer levels to ascend and often feature a suite of amenities that rival some luxury resorts.

EPILOGUE: CHOOSING YOUR LAS VEGAS ABODE

As we draw the curtains on this chapter, remember that whether you opt for the solitary splendor of a single-family home, the communal charm of a garden-style apartment, or the elevated existence of a mid-rise, Las Vegas offers a range of living experiences as diverse as the attractions that line its famed Strip.

The Las Vegas residential real estate market reflects not just the city's architectural diversity but also its unique position as a place of both permanent residence and fleeting pleasure. In any city, your choice in habitat is something of a gamble, but, as any Vegas veteran will tell you, the most astute players—be they renters or buyers—often find a way to beat the odds and come out on top.

7.   THE MOVING PROCESS

The tale of moving houses is often told in hushed tones, akin to recounting an epic journey across turbulent seas; in our case, it's the traversal to the heart of the desert where neon reigns supreme—Las Vegas. It requires a plan, patience, and perhaps a predilection for slight madness. Let us delve deeper, shall we?

THE MASTER PLAN: DRAWING THE MAP

Embarking on your journey to Las Vegas begins not with suitcases but with a meticulous battle plan, charted as if laying siege to a medieval fortress, though this particular fortress beckons with LED lights, modern amenities, and palm trees.

Inventory Re-assessment: Delve deep into your possessions. Question the existential necessity of each item. This step is crucial, as the weight of your belongings directly correlates to the cost of your move. Each item jettisoned becomes a badge of honor, simplifying the journey to your new home.

Mark Your Calendars: Begin early. Marking your timeline affords you the luxury of spreading out tasks, thus avoiding the last-minute pandemonium that often accompanies moving. A wisely-charted calendar is the beacon that guides you through the stormy waters of relocation.

Choosing Your Companions: Also known as "The Moving Company Chronicles," herein lies the heart of your saga. Picking a moving company is akin to selecting your fellowship for a journey through Middle Earth, minus the orcs but fraught with its own perils.

Research and Reviews: Dive into the depths of the internet. Seek companies bathed in the glowing reviews of past travelers.

Remember, around 35.5 million Americans embark on a move each year. Their tales—of valor and victory versus despair and defeat—can help pave the path for your journey. Companies replete with accreditation from the American Moving and Storage Association are your knights in shining armor.

Quotes Galore: Solicit at least three in-person estimates. Any mover offering a quote from afar, sight unseen, is akin to a fortune teller promising riches—enticing but invariably dubious. These estimates are your compass, ensuring you don't wander into financial wilderness. Remember, in trying to predict moving expenses, include tips for the moving crew, or any additional costs arising from changes in volume or time estimates.

Licensing and Defense: Ensure your chosen brigade is licensed and insured. The knights entrusted with all your earthly possessions should be sheathed in the armor of legitimacy.

PACKING: THE ARTIFACT ASSEMBLY

Packing is a ritual, a rite of passage marking the transition from one realm to another. It's an art form, really—one fraught with nostalgia, strategy, and inevitable frustrations.

Gathering Supplies: Arm yourself with an arsenal of packing tape, sturdy boxes, bubble wrap, and, importantly, a functioning Sharpie. When the quest for the coffee maker doesn't turn into an excavation mission, you'll be glad you did.

Logical Packing: Approach this task as a grand strategy game. Items seldom used are banished to the boxes first. Label with the precision of an archivist. A box marked "Stuff" is a trap for future frustration.

Essentials Kit: Assemble a treasure chest of essentials, a "go bag," if you will—medications, toiletries, important documents, fresh attire for a few days, and provisions (snacks are non-negotiable). This kit is your lifeline amidst the chaos of moving.

THE GRAND ARRIVAL: SETTLING INTO THE SHIMMERING SANDS

The day of days arrives with all the pomp and circumstance of a royal coronation—at least as far as you're concerned. The caravan bearing your worldly possessions pulls up in front of your new home, and the unloading begins. This moment, this day, is the first page of the next chapter that is your life in Las Vegas.

Final Coordination: Make sure to have a chat ahead of time with the building folks to see if they've got a bunch of rules about booking the freight elevator, any ticking clock on how long you can use it, certain days of the week that are off-limits, or paperwork like insurance certifications and other such approvals that need filling out in advance.

Direction and Oversight: Welcome the moving company with the grace of a seasoned general overseeing your troops. Direct them with clarity, ensuring each box finds its appointed chamber within your new abode.

The Final Inspection: Before departing your former castle you will have conducted a thorough survey. Check every closet, every nook, and make sure you're not leaving behind anything valuable, sentimental, or essential behind.

Unpacking with Intent: Approach unpacking as one might approach herding a pack of large, heavy, sluggish animals. Start with the essentials, moving them into their designated places, gradually building a life in your new home. The sooner you unpack, the better—that herd isn't going to migrate by itself.

Exploration Awaits: Once the dust settles—or when you desperately need a break from unpacking—step out into the embrace of Las Vegas, a city vibrant with life, waiting to be discovered.

EPILOGUE: IN THE GLOW OF THE NEON

With your new domicile as a home base, the adventure truly begins. Las Vegas, with its promise of unrestrained liberty and boundless opportunity, beckons. The city, vast and sprawling, is now your playground, your home. For visitors at the casinos, fortunes can turn on the flip of a card or the roll of a dice—but because of your meticulous planning and strategic moving, you're already holding the winning hand.

8. LEGAL AND ADMINISTRATIVE TASKS

Welcome, dear reader, to what is considered the less exciting side of relocation—and in fact, of pretty much any venture: legal and administrative tasks. If moving were a Las Vegas show, this chapter would be the fine print on the back of your ticket stub, the terms and conditions of your grand adventure. Important, yes, but far less thrilling than the main event.

A NEW IDENTITY IN THE NEON WILDERNESS

Relocating to Las Vegas isn't just about swapping out your backdrop for desert skies and palm trees—it also means updating those the plastic cards and reams of paper that confirm you are who you say you are.

UPDATING IDS—A RITE OF PASSAGE

Moving to Nevada means you'll need to update your driver's license to a shiny new one adorned with the state's insignia. The state decrees that you've got 30 days to trade in your old ID at the Department of Motor Vehicles (DMV). Fail to meet this deadline, and you are gambling with your own mobility in a place where cars serve as the main form of transportation.

Did you know that DMV wait times can rival that of the most popular brunch spots in Vegas on a Sunday? It's true (and the DMV doesn't even serve food!). Making an appointment can save you from taking up a new residence—in the waiting room. Consult the Nevada DMV website (see below) for a checklist of what you need to bring, which will include proof of identity and residency, as well as a day's supply of patience.

Nevada DMV: For the closest DMV office, appointment reservations, and the list of documents you'll need, visit www.dmvnv.com or call the Contact Center at (702) 486-4DMV (4368).

REGISTERING YOUR CHARIOT

Your vehicle also needs to don the local armor—new license plates. This task dances hand-in-hand with getting a new license, ensnaring you in the DMV's version of the tango (or is it... the limbo?). Vehicles are to be registered within 30 days of moving, saving you from potential citations or puzzled looks when you explain why your car is still pledging allegiance to another state—one in which it *snows*, no less.

Vehicle Registration Info: Dive into the DMV's treasure trove of information at dmvnv.com or via their helpline for specifics on transitioning your car's registration.

THE GREAT UTILITY TRANSFER

Transitioning utilities to your new Vegas abode is a task that sits somewhere between "utterly mundane" and "vitally important." Before the moving truck even pulls up, you'll want lights to flick on and water to gush forth at your command—and with some pre-planning, you can make this a reality. Contacting the local utility companies before your move allows you to arrange service start dates. In Las Vegas, the water you drink and the electricity that lights your life are likely supplied by the Las Vegas Valley Water District and NV Energy, respectively. A pro tip: Paying any outstanding bills and notifying your former providers of your move will prevent any haunting past-due notices.

Power: For electricity, NV Energy stands ready to illuminate your path. Reach them at nvenergy.com or call 702-402-5555.

Water: The Las Vegas Valley Water District will keep you hydrated. Wade through their resources at lvvwd.com or quench your informational thirst by calling 702-870-4194.

MAIL FORWARDING: BECAUSE BILLS TRAVEL TOO

The United States Postal Service, that stalwart carrier of letters and parcels, offers a simple online form to ensure your mail follows you into the desert. This digital breadcrumb trail costs less than a cup of coffee at most establishments, ensuring that from bills to birthday cards, everything finds its way to you.

U.S. Postal Service: Change your address online at www.usps.com or visit your nearest post office.

INSURANCE: THE SAFETY NET FOR YOUR NEW TIGHTROPE WALK

Updating your insurance policies is akin to checking your safety harness before a high-wire act. From health to auto and home or renter's insurance, ensuring coverage in your new digs is crucial. A delightful quirk of insurance is its locality dependency—rates can fluctuate based on your new address. Consulting with your insurance agents pre-move can avert any coverage catastrophes post-relocation.

When it comes to auto insurance, the move to Las Vegas introduces an essential requirement. The state of Nevada mandates that drivers secure their auto insurance from an agency licensed to operate within the state. This is not merely a procedural formality; it's a safeguard that ensures your policy complies with the specific legal and coverage demands of Nevada. The state sets forth minimum coverage requirements that are non-negotiable: $25,000 for bodily injury or death of one person in any one accident; $50,000 for bodily injury or death of two or more persons in any one accident; and $20,000 for injury to or destruction of property of others in any one accident. These figures underscore the state's commitment to ensuring that all drivers carry sufficient protection to cover the unforeseen, yet potentially substantial, costs of accidents.

VOTING: BECAUSE EVERY VOICE COUNTS, EVEN IN THE DESERT

Lastly, let's not forget about registering to vote. Becoming part of the civic process in Nevada allows you to have a say in everything from local referendums to who becomes the nation's president. Given the state's occasionally pivotal role in national elections, your ballot could be the metaphorical butterfly whose wings incite a hurricane of change. Voter registration can often be completed while updating your ID at the DMV, killing two bureaucratic birds with one stone, albeit a very slow stone.

Voter Registration: DMV, or visit www.registertovotenv.gov for online registration.

In the grand patchwork quilt that is relocation, these tasks form the essential, albeit unglamorous, stitches that hold the adventure together. While they might not pulse with the excitement of, say, your first night spent on the Strip, they are the foundation upon which your new life in Las Vegas is built. Consider this chapter your map through the bureaucratic maze—a guide to ensure that, as you forsake your former resident status for that of a bonafide Las Vegan, you do so with all the t's crossed and i's dotted.

EPILOGUE: SETTING THE STAGE

As we lower the curtain on the less dazzling chapter of legal and administrative tasks, let's not forget there's a peculiar charm to these rites of passage. Consider the DMV not as a dreary checkpoint, but as the first thrilling pit stop in the race through your new Las Vegas life. Yes, updating IDs and registering vehicles might lack the excitement promised by living Las Vegas, but these are the very acts that will help cement your status as a resident of the city.

These administrative tasks are your own personal metamorphosis in a place famed for its own dramatic transformations. They help the unfamiliar become the familiar, and turn the visitor into a resident. Vegas, after all, is a place where every detail, no matter how small, contributes to the larger spectacle of your adventure.

9.   EDUCATION AND SCHOOLS

Over the years, Las Vegas has committed to providing its residents with a surprisingly diverse and sprawling educational landscape, ranging from the spirited playgrounds of public schools to the hallowed halls of higher education.

THE PUBLIC ARENA: MORE THAN JUST A ROLL OF THE DICE

At first, venturing into the world of public education in Las Vegas can feel akin to sitting down at a vast, somewhat bewildering gaming table. The Clark County School District (CCSD)—the largest in the state and the fifth-largest in the nation—is the dealer here, overseeing this complex and high-stakes game.

With more than 300,000 students spread across roughly 380 schools, the diversity in this district mirrors that of Las Vegas itself, with schools varying widely in size, programs, and resources. (For more details, their website CCSD.net provides a wealth of information.)

School zones are created with a simple goal: to keep your mini-scholars in a school that's a stone's throw away from home—that would be the district. The area designated for a child's school increases with age. For the little ones in elementary, the zone hugs close to home, cozy as a backyard. But as they sprout up to high school age, the zone stretches its legs, sprawling out like a teenager on a sofa, and covering a much grander expanse. The district, in a juggling act worthy of a Cirque du Soleil performance, tries to keep these zones compact while ensuring no school is bursting at the seams. The CCSD's website offers zone maps crafted with the precision of a Swiss watch. Parents can enter their address and—voilà —the zoned school appears.

Public schools in Las Vegas, like anywhere, run the gamut from those that struggle to hit the jackpot in terms of performance and resources to those that are flush with innovative programs, top-tier educators, and facilities that would make some colleges envious.

The district has a variety of programs aimed at enhancing educational outcomes, such ReInvent Schools Las Vegas. There are also some highly rated schools in the district, like Vanderburg John Elementary School and Vassiliadis Billy & Rosemary Elementary School.

However, the district faces significant challenges. A 2021 report ranked the Las Vegas region as the second-worst for school quality among the nation's 50 largest metropolitan areas. The district has also been grappling with a teacher shortage, which has increased by 50% since 2020. This deficit has led to classes being canceled or combined, impacting the learning environment.

The district is also dealing with funding issues. A 2022 study found that Nevada public schools are the most poorly funded in the country. This lack of funding impacts the resources available to students and teachers, and ultimately, the quality of education.

A survey taken by Clark County students shows that safety perceptions vary across schools. CCSD has implemented safety measures and works closely with local law enforcement agencies to ensure school safety. Efforts to improve safety include addressing teacher retention and having community advocates like Dads in Schools provide an additional adult presence.

But the district is committed to improving. The district's five-year strategic plan, Focus: 2024, aims to ensure equity and access to a rich and rigorous education for all students. The CCSD reported a graduation rate of 81.5% for the classes of 2023, which is an increase from the previous year and higher than the statewide graduation rate. Magnet schools, charter schools and the Nevada State High School throw interesting cards into the mix.

Charter Schools: These institutions are the mavericks of the public school system, operating with a significant degree of autonomy. Each school deals its own hand, focusing on diverse educational philosophies or specialized programs, from STEM to the arts. They're publicly funded but independently run, an interesting bet for families looking for a distinct educational model outside the traditional public system.

Magnet Schools: A magnet in more ways than one, these schools draw students based on specific learning focuses. Whether it's science and technology, performing arts, or international studies, magnet schools attract students keen on honing their skills and passions. They aim to bring together a diverse student body from across different demographics, promoting integration and specialized learning. The Clark County School District (CCSD) oversees numerous magnet programs, each designed as a beacon for those with focused academic or artistic inclinations. magnet.ccsd.net

Nevada State High School (NSHS): Nevada State High School is where high school meets college in a unique educational mash-up. Students here are not just tackling the usual high school fare; they're also diving into college courses. It's a dual journey where they earn both high school diplomas and college credits, setting them on a fast track to higher education. Think of it as a two-for-one educational deal, blending teenage life with a collegiate leap forward.

NOT ALL SCHOOLS ARE CREATED EQUAL: COMPARING SCHOOLS

Embarking on the quest to evaluate Las Vegas public schools before you've even chosen what neighborhood to live in is a little like choosing the perfect show to see before you hit the Strip—granted, the stakes are different, but it's an important step that will shape your entire experience. Since you're still in the planning stages of your move, you're not tethered to any school zone or haunted by commute times. Once you've zeroed in on the perfect school, you can then scout for a home within its gravitational pull. Here's how to play the sleuth in the schoolyard:

The Numbers Game: The Nevada Report Card offers detailed insights into standardized test scores, graduation rates, and other crucial metrics. The Nevada Department of Education utilizes the Nevada School Performance Framework (NSPF) to assess each school's performance. nevadareportcard.nv.gov/di/

The Word on the Street: Sites like www.GreatSchools.org and www.Niche.com are like Yelp for education, offering unfiltered reviews from those on the front lines—parents and students.

The Recon Mission: Nothing beats the old "boots on the ground" approach. Visiting schools is like a backstage tour, offering a real feel for the place beyond glossy brochures.

THE GREAT PAPER CHASE: SCHOOL REGISTRATION DOCUMENTS

Ah, the joyous occasion of school registration, where gathering documents resembles a scavenger hunt meticulously crafted by bureaucrats with a fondness for paperwork. As a newcomer to the CCSD, your journey begins with online registration at ccsd.net/parents/enrollment/zoning (be sure to check the "new to district" section). This step is essential for all schooling levels—elementary, middle, and high school. Once you've completed the online registration application, make your way to your child's zoned school with all the required documents in hand:

Your ID: Personal identification of parent/guardian such as driver's license or passport bearing your name.

Child's ID: You will need only one of these documents. Remember, originals only—no photocopies:

- An original birth certificate.
- A passport.
- Certified birth card issued by the Clark County Health District or another health district.
- We'll say it again: originals only—no photocopies.

Immunization Record: The immunization history of your child.

Address Verification: You'll need one of these:

- Recent utility bill
- Rent receipt
- Residence Lease or Sales Contract

A little caveat: if you're brandishing a sales contract for a new home, the school will let you in, but expects another proof of address within 30 days. And before you ask: the answer is no, a driver's license, telephone bill, or cable bill won't do the trick.

MAGNET SCHOOLS: THE QUEST FOR ADMISSION

Securing a position in one of these coveted institutions is akin to striking gold in the Nevada desert. The process begins with the Clark County School District (CCSD) Open Enrollment period, typically launching in the fall. Hopeful students and their guardians embark on a quest, armed with curiosity and driven by the dream of specialized education.

The Exploration: The first leg of the journey involves exploration. In this phase, families navigate through the plethora of options. Each magnet school showcases unique programs designed to cater to various academic interests and talents. For instance, the Las Vegas Academy of the Arts dances to the beat of its own drum, quite literally, focusing on the performing and visual arts, while the Advanced Technologies Academy delves into the realms of computer science and engineering wizardry.

Open House Adventures: Open houses, typically held between October and January, are crucial for gathering information. They offer insights into the school environment and curriculum and are opportunities to interact with teachers and staff.

The Application Process: The application period usually opens in October and closes in mid-January for the following school year. It's an online process via the CCSD Magnet Schools website at magnet.ccsd.net. Parents can apply to up to three schools, ranking them in order of preference. Late applications open in Mid-March. Remember, late applications are like arriving to a show after the curtain rises—you might still get a seat, but it's a bit of a gamble.

The Lottery: Yes, you read that right. The allocation of spots in these hallowed halls involves a lottery system, in the grand tradition of Las Vegas being a city of chance. However, unlike the rolling dice at a craps table, this lottery is computer-generated, ensuring fairness and transparency. Factors like having a sibling in the same school, residing in a less advantaged zone, or applying to less popular programs can improve your odds. Geographic preferences give local students a better shot at attending nearby schools, whether it's because they live near the school or in designated transportation zones. In February or March, the magical algorithm decides the fate of thousands, allocating spots based on the number of applications and available seats.

The Waiting Game: After applying, it's a bit like waiting for a pot to boil. Keep an eye on your email—and remember, sometimes important stuff hides in the spam folder. Keep looking; it's like checking the time, but more fun. Notifications are sent out in April. Possible outcomes:

- Selected: Congratulations, you've hit the jackpot! Now, just follow the yellow brick road (also known as the registration instructions).

- Alternate Pool: It's like being on standby for a flight to somewhere amazing. Patience is key, and crossing your fingers never hurts.

- Not Qualified: If this is you, don't despair. It's not the end—it's just a plot twist. Offers can be made up until the second week of the following school year.

Where to Turn for Help: Applying to a Las Vegas magnet school is a bet worth placing for its unique educational opportunities. The process, though daunting, can lead to an exceptional educational experience for your child. Navigating this route can be challenging, but there are resources:

- CCSD Magnet School Office: For guidance and specific queries. Contact at (702) 799-8492 or through their website.

- School Counselors: They offer insights into the application process and preparation for tests or auditions.

- Parent Workshops: CCSD provides these workshops for information about the application process and choosing the right program.

GIFTED AND TALENTED SERVICES: NURTURING THE BRIGHT LIGHTS

Programs aimed at gifted and talented students are designed to cater to these bright young minds, and offer more than just accelerated learning; they provide a greenhouse for intellectual, creative, and leadership potential.

The CCSD's Gifted and Talented Education (GATE) program is where these bright lights are given the chance to shine even brighter, challenging their abilities and providing opportunities for advancement that match their exceptional capabilities. ssd.ccsd.net/gifted-education-services/

SPECIAL EDUCATION: EVERY STUDENT CAN SHINE

Inclusion is the keyword in Las Vegas's educational system, ensuring that every student, regardless of their personal hurdles, has the opportunity to succeed and find their own spotlight.

Special Education Services within CCSD are comprehensive, offering a spectrum of support from early childhood intervention to transition programs for older students. These programs are tailored to meet a wide array of needs, so that every student has access to the tools and resources necessary for their optimal development.

THE PRIVATE SCHOOL BET: WAGERING ON A SURE THING?

For those who prefer an alternative to public education, Las Vegas offers a hand of private institutions, each with its unique deck. From faith-based scholastic sanctuaries to avant-garde academies dedicated to the arts and sciences, private education in Las Vegas caters to a myriad of learning philosophies and preferences. Notable contenders:

The Meadows School: College admissions highlights include enrollments into prestigious universities such as Columbia, Cornell, Dartmouth, Duke, and Yale. Offers 30 AP and Advanced Topics classes. 27% of the class of 2023 recognized by National Merit Scholarship competition.

Bishop Gorman High School: 2023 graduates have matriculated into colleges such as CalTech, Carnegie Mellon, MIT, Princeton, and Stanford. Offers 25 AP courses. The class of 2023 had 13 National Merit Commended Students, ten Finalists, and one Recipient.

Faith Lutheran Middle & High School: Graduates have gained acceptance into colleges such as Harvard, John Hopkins, MIT, Princeton, Stanford, and Yale. Offers 36 honors and 21 AP courses. 3 students in the class of 2023 had a perfect ACT score (36).

Lake Mead Christian Academy: Recent graduates have been accepted into prestigious colleges such as Carnegie Mellon, Columbia, Stanford, UC Berkeley, and UCLA. Offers honors, AP, and dual enrollment options. Graduates have been offered over $2 million in scholarships over the last three years.

The Adelson Educational Campus: Members of the Class of 2022 & 2023 gained acceptance into highly-selective colleges such as Brown, Cornell, Duke, Johns Hopkins, Stanford, and Yale. 76% of students score a 3 or higher on AP tests. The Class of 2023 included three National Merit Scholarship Qualifiers.

What's the wager? Private education comes at a price, with tuition costs as variable as the games on the casino floor from $13,000 to $30,000. However, for many families, the tailored educational experiences and often smaller class sizes are worth the ante.

THE COLLEGIATE QUEST: BEYOND THE BACHELOR'S

As for higher education, Las Vegas is more than a mere blip on the academic radar. The city is home to institutions that cater to a wide spectrum of scholarly pursuits, from vocational training to advanced research degrees.

University of Nevada, Las Vegas (UNLV): As the flagship higher education institution in the city, UNLV offers an array of undergraduate, graduate, and professional programs. Nestled close to the heart of Las Vegas, it serves as a vibrant hub of research, innovation, and higher learning. Explore more at unlv.edu

Nevada State College (NSC): A bit younger and smaller, this institution prides itself on a more intimate learning environment and a strong emphasis on teaching excellence. Its growing campus and expanding program offerings continue to enrich the region's educational tapestry. Visit nsc.edu for further enlightenment.

The College of Southern Nevada (CSN): As one of the largest public colleges in the United States, CSN is a cornerstone of Las Vegas's educational foundation, providing vocational training, associate degrees, and a pathway to a four-year education. Its offerings are as diverse as the city itself. Delve into the possibilities at csn.edu

LIFELONG LEARNING: THE UNENDING QUEST FOR KNOWLEDGE

Las Vegas shines not only for those seeking formal education—the city teems with opportunities for lifelong learners to explore new passions, refine skills, or pivot careers entirely. From culinary arts that reflect the city's renowned dining scene to innovative tech courses driven by Las Vegas's burgeoning tech sector, the city truly understands that education never really ends.

Culinary Arts: Imagine a place where your taste buds tingle at the mere mention of its name—enter Las Vegas, a veritable feast for the culinary curious. Dreaming of a spatula in one hand and a whisk in the other amidst the hustle and bustle of Sin City? The Culinary Academy of Las Vegas isn't merely a cooking school; it's your golden ticket to the culinary big leagues, offering courses in everything from sautéing to soufflés in the heart of one of the planet's most pulsating food scenes.

Technology and Innovation: The Las Vegas tech scene is brimming with digital dreams and silicon aspirations. The University of Nevada, Las Vegas (UNLV) stands as a beacon for budding technophiles with programs like cybersecurity, emerging technologies, and innovation. Not to mention, with every tech meetup and hackathon, including the star-studded annual CES, you're not just attending an event; you're plugging directly into the future.

Hospitality and Gaming Management: In a city that wrote the book on entertainment and relaxation, Las Vegas boasts educational powerhouses in hospitality and gaming management. The William F. Harrah College of Hospitality at UNLV goes way beyond textbooks and lectures, offering a backstage pass to the world's most dazzling hospitality stage and real-world tutorials on how to wow guests and manage casinos, right at the source.

Arts and Entertainment: For the creatively inclined, Las Vegas rolls out the red carpet. At the Las Vegas Academy of the Arts, students don't just study art—they breathe, eat, and live it. Meanwhile, the city's smorgasbord of galleries, theaters, and music venues serve not only as monuments to human creativity but as classrooms for the next generation of artists, offering a chorus of workshops and seminars to fine-tune your craft or dance to the rhythm of your passion.

Health and Wellness: Whether you're aspiring to master the downward-facing dog or blend the perfect nutritional smoothie, Las Vegas offers a sanctuary for those eager to teach, learn, or talk about well-being. With a myriad of programs from yoga teacher training to holistic health seminars, the city invites you to embark on a journey of personal enlightenment and professional growth amidst the neon lights.

EPILOGUE: BRIGHT MINDS, BRIGHTER LIGHTS

The vibrant educational landscape in Las Vegas offers a jackpot of learning opportunities for all ages. From the dynamic public schools of the Clark County School District to specialized magnet and charter schools, Las Vegas presents the option of varied academic pathways, each promising a bright future for its students.

Choosing an educational path in this city is less a gamble and more a strategic decision, with each option setting the stage for lifelong success. As our exploration concludes, know that Las Vegas is not just a city of entertainment but a hub of learning and growth, where the odds are always in favor of those who seek knowledge.

10.   HEALTHCARE AND SAFETY

Ah, Las Vegas—a city that dazzles with the luminous glow of a thousand suns (if those suns were made of neon and powered by an endless supply of electricity). The city is an emblem of entertainment, indulgence, and—let's face it—a bit of chaos. But amidst the roulette wheels and poker tables, there lies a robust backbone of healthcare facilities, emergency services, and safety nets. Because even adventurers need a plan for when the unexpected happens, don't they?

HEALTHCARE FACILITIES: MORE THAN JUST A LUCKY CHARM

Las Vegas boasts an impressive array of healthcare facilities ranging from sprawling hospitals to specialized clinics. The city's healthcare landscape is characterized by a mix of challenges common to rapidly growing cities and significant advancements in medical care and infrastructure.

Setting up an appointment with a primary care doctor in Las Vegas can feel a bit like planning a night out on the Strip—lots of logistics. Availability can swing wildly depending on the healthcare provider, how many other people are trying to get in, and just how the clinics like to do things. Imagine trying to get into the hottest club without a reservation!

For those seeking VIP healthcare, concierge medicine offers a more personalized approach. By paying an upfront fee, either monthly or annually, you enjoy head-of-the-line privileges, ensuring prioritized access and more one-on-one time with your doctor. However, remember concierge medicine is an add-on, not a substitute for medical insurance. Costs range from about $1,500 to $3,000 annually.

Nevada was ranked 31st overall in healthcare by U.S. News & World Reports and 23rd in terms of the cost of healthcare by Wallet Hub. The city's healthcare sector makes up 9.5% of its economy, indicating its significance beyond tourism. Las Vegas is home to many quality hospitals that are well-distributed geographically, ensuring accessible healthcare for residents.

University Medical Center (UMC): As the pinnacle of health services in the region and at the forefront of medical care, UMC is in the heart of Las Vegas, and known for its trauma center—one of the best in the country—skill, dedication, and continuing growth take center stage. www.umcsn.com

Elite Medical Center: Elite Medical Center is open 24/7 and provides adult and pediatric emergency care, trauma and injury care, cardiology services, imaging, and lab services. It is known for its high-rated patient satisfaction and offers a wide range of services, including inpatient medical services and patient care. The hospital is also the first in Nevada to be accredited to administer Zulresso, a groundbreaking treatment for postpartum depression. It accepts most private and commercial insurance, including Medicare. elitelv.com

Centennial Hills Hospital Medical Center: Part of the Valley Health System, Centennial Hills Hospital Medical Center has received numerous awards and accreditations from government medical societies and other groups. www.centennialhillshospital.com

Cleveland Clinic Lou Ruvo Center for Brain Health: Focused on providing top-tier care for neurological disorders, this facility combines futuristic architecture with cutting-edge medicine. It's a place where science fiction meets medical reality, and it stands as a testament to Las Vegas's commitment to health innovation. my.clevelandclinic.org/locations/lou-ruvo-center-for-brain-health

WILDLIFE: NATURE'S UNPREDICTABLE NEIGHBOR

Just as the glittering lights of the Vegas Strip illuminate the night, the area's wildlife adds a touch of wild wonder to the desert landscape. Living in Las Vegas means sharing your surroundings with a variety of desert creatures, from the humble roadrunner to the elusive scorpion. These natural neighbors, though often unseen, play a crucial role in the desert ecosystem.

While the city's hustle and bustle may seem worlds away from nature, residents often find themselves crossing paths with these creatures. Scorpions and spiders, in particular, are a common sight, especially in suburban areas bordering natural habitats. If this sort of thing bugs you, read on to learn how to identify—and avoid—these creepy crawlies.

Scorpions, known for their stinging tail, are as much a part of Vegas as the casinos themselves. The Bark Scorpion is notoriously known for its potent venom, this scorpion is easily identified by its long, slender tail and pincers. The Desert Hairy Scorpion is larger but less venomous, this species is recognized by its hairy body and larger pincers.

When it comes to spiders, the black widow and brown recluse are notable for their venom and tendency to dwell close to human habitats. The black widow is easily identified by its jet-black, round body and distinctive red hourglass marking on its underside. The brown recluse, on the other hand, is recognized by its smaller body and long, spindly legs.

Safety Tips for Coexisting with Wildlife:

Elevated Living: For those wary of scorpions and spiders, choosing mid-rise buildings over single-family homes or garden style apartments can be a safer option.

Vigilance is Key: Regularly inspect and seal your home to prevent these critters from entering.

Professional Assistance: If you encounter a black widow or brown recluse, do not attempt to handle it yourself. Instead, back away and contact professional pest control services.

Light the Way: Outdoor lighting can help deter nocturnal wildlife.

Education Matters: Learn to identify local wildlife, particularly venomous species, and understand how to avoid them.

Respecting and understanding the wildlife in Las Vegas, including scorpions and these venomous spiders, is crucial for a harmonious and safe coexistence with nature's unpredictable neighbors. And remember, they're just as scared of you...

CRIME: THE UNWANTED HOUSEGUEST

Like an uninvited guest who crashes the party and refuses to leave, crime has a way of showing up where it's least welcome. Las Vegas, even with its round-the-clock lifestyle and high volume of tourists, isn't immune to the trials and tribulations that come with urban living. From the Strip's crowded sidewalks to the quiet suburban streets, the city experiences its share of unlawful shenanigans.

The crime rates, it must be noted, are a bit like casino odds—they fluctuate. While some areas of Las Vegas are as serene as a morning in the desert, others can feel as risky as betting it all on red. Property crime, including burglary and auto theft, often takes center stage, reminding residents and visitors to keep their wits about them. Maintaining safety in Las Vegas, then, is less about eschewing the city's allure and more about using common sense and adopting a balanced approach to urban living:

Community Camaraderie: Engage with your neighborhood. Whether it's attending local meetings or simply getting to know your neighbors, a connected community is a safer one.

Secure Your Sanctuary: Invest in good locks, security systems, and outdoor lighting. In a city that never sleeps, let your home be your safe haven. If you're renting, make sure to bring any concerns to your landlord (and check your lease so you know what security measures are part of the agreement).

Report and Support: Be proactive in reporting suspicious activities. In Las Vegas, where the unusual can sometimes seem ordinary, it's better to err on the side of caution.

Hide thy Treasures: Las Vegas might not have pirates, but it's still wise to safeguard your valuables. A money belt, for example, isn't just a fashion statement—it can mean peace of mind.

Stay Illuminated: Stick to well-lit routes, especially at night. Not only is it safer, but you'll also get to enjoy the city's famous lights in all their glory.

In closing, it's important to note that Las Vegas, for all its flamboyance and flair, is not so different from any other city when it comes to crime. The key to enjoying the best of what it has to offer lies in preparation, awareness, and good old-fashioned common sense.

GENERAL SAFETY TIPS: PLAYING IT SAFE IN SIN CITY

Living in the Mojave comes with a certain level of risk, much like playing the slots. There are flash floods, which can turn dry creek beds into raging rivers faster than you can say "I won!" Dust storms can make driving as hazardous as navigating the blackjack table after a few too many cocktails.

Then there's the heat. Summer temperatures can soar above 115°F, turning cars into ovens and sidewalks into frying pans. Wildfires are a threat in the nearby forests during dry conditions. And let's not forget the local wildlife—critters such as rattlesnakes, scorpions, black widow spiders, and centipedes can sound a little bit like the lineup of a very effective horror movie.

Being prepared is key. Pay attention to weather forecasts, exercise caution outdoors, and make sure your home is safe from these natural hazards. Living in—or even just visiting—any big city requires a pinch of caution and a dash of common sense.

Stay Hydrated: The Nevada desert isn't kidding around with its heat. Carrying water is an absolute must for tourists and locals alike.

Know Your Limits: Whether it's gambling, partying, or sunbathing, moderation is your friend in a city built on exuberant excess.

Be Street Smart: Keep belongings close, especially on crowded sidewalks and casinos; pickpockets thrive on a chaotic, target-rich environment.

Use Trusted Transportation: Stick to licensed taxis, public transportation, or established options; the few extra dollars beat getting lost or worse.

EMERGENCY SERVICES: THE UNSUNG HEROES OF THE ENTERTAINMENT CAPITAL

When the going gets tough, or when what happened in Vegas didn't quite stay in Vegas (and involved a trip to the ER), the city's emergency services stand ready to leap into action.

Las Vegas Fire & Rescue (LVF&R): With stations strategically scattered throughout the valley, these are the folks who battle blazes, respond to medical emergencies, and essentially keep the pulse of the city beating hearty and healthy. fire.lasvegasnevada.gov

Las Vegas Metropolitan Police Department (LVMPD): Maintaining law and order and keeping crime at bay (excluding crimes of fashion or the heart), the LVMPD is a force to be reckoned with. They're the thin blue line ensuring that the city's wild heart doesn't skip a beat. www.lvmpd.com

EPILOGUE: SAFEGUARDING THE GLITTER

In Las Vegas, beneath the shimmering veneer of midnight revelries and casino chimes, beats a heart attuned to the well-being and safety of its dwellers and guests. The city's healthcare facilities stand as modern-day temples to science and wellness, emergency services operate with clockwork precision to safeguard the populace, and a few simple safety tips ensure that your Las Vegas story is one of joy and returned deposits.

As the sun sets on the Nevada desert each evening, it's comforting to know that in Las Vegas, whether you're enjoying the highs or facing the lows, there's always a network of professionals and services ready to ensure your journey is one with a happy ending.

11.   TRANSPORTATION AND COMMUTING

Navigating the streets, freeways, and thoroughfares of Las Vegas can feel like participating in a high-stakes game of chance where the grand prize is arriving at the correct destination on time. Let's roll the dice and explore the avenues (both literal and metaphorical) of moving around in this desert metropolis.

FROM A TO B: THE ROADS OF CHANCE

By Car: In Vegas, the automobile is king, queen, and the occasional joker. The freedom to zip from the neon glow of Fremont Street to the tranquil outskirts of the city demands a personal vehicle. However, this freedom comes with the caveat of traffic, a beast as unpredictable as a slot machine and just as likely to test your patience. The secret to taming this beast lies in understanding the rhythms of the city and planning accordingly. Rush hour in Vegas, much like its nightlife, can be both exhilarating and exasperating. However, it's still much better than the traffic in Los Angeles or San Francisco.

Public Transit: For those seeking an alternative to the vehicular ballet, the Regional Transportation Commission of Southern Nevada (RTC) serves as the master choreographer of public transport. Buses, the workhorses of the RTC fleet, offer an inexpensive (sometimes even free!) and reliable—if not always swift—means of traversing the cityscape.

The RTC offers a network of bus routes that weave across the valley, like threads in a vast tapestry. These include:

- Local routes for basic neighborhood service
- "The Deuce" route, connecting Downtown resorts and attractions

- Strip & Downtown Express (SDX) for a faster journey along the Strip and to the airport

- Residential commuter routes that whisk suburbanites to places like Summerlin

Fares are a bargain at just $2 per local ride, with discounts available for seniors, youth, and disabled riders. Value passes are the ace in the hole for frequent users.

While buses run from 5 am to 2 am daily, weekends can see wait times stretching to 30 minutes—a small eternity in a city that never stops moving. Nevertheless, for those dependent on transit, a combination of routes can get you almost anywhere in the city, albeit with a bit of patience and planning. For schedules, routes, and mystical incantations to ensure your bus arrives on time, visit www.rtcsnv.com

The Monorail and Beyond: Gliding above the fray, the Las Vegas Monorail is the city's nod to the future—a sleek, elevated train offering expansive views and a respite from the congestion below. It's a favorite for those venturing along the Strip, providing not just transport but an experience. Meanwhile, services like the Downtown Loop provide a complimentary ride through the heart of Las Vegas, proving that sometimes, the best things in life (or at least in transit) really are free.

Biking and Walking: In certain sanctuaries within the city, particularly the blissfully pedestrian-friendly District at Green Valley or the Arts District, traveling on foot or by bike is not only viable but pleasant. Here, the world unfolds at a stroller's pace, revealing the intricacies of Las Vegas life often missed at higher speeds. While bike lanes might be as rare as a quiet night on the Strip, there are several scenic trails that offer a respite from the motorized chaos:

- The River Mountains Loop Trail offers a scenic 35-mile bike path through Henderson.

- West Flamingo Trail and Tropicana Wash Trail provide links from Summerlin to the Strip.

- Henderson boasts over 75 miles of on-street and pathway trails connecting various neighborhoods.

- Dedicated bike lanes on Casino Center Blvd ensure safe passage to Downtown.

As in any city, cyclists should exercise caution on busy roads, remain visible at all times, and securely lock their bikes in high-theft areas. Additionally, the hot summer weather demands extra attention to hydration and sun protection. However, with optimal weather, cycling in Las Vegas can be a truly enjoyable way to get around.

DRIVING: A TEST OF WITS AND PATIENCE

Driving in Las Vegas can often feel like participating in an elaborate motorized ballet, albeit one choreographed by someone with a rather cruel sense of humor. The local highways—the mighty Interstates 15, 215, 515, and the ever-busy US 95—are the lifeblood of the city, pulsating with a constant flow of vehicles. Navigating these roads requires the patience of a saint and the reflexes of a Formula 1 driver, especially during those peak hours when traffic moves with all the haste of a sloth.

Imagine, if you will, standing at the nexus of possibility—or more accurately, at the spaghetti bowl interchange of I-15 and US 95 in downtown Las Vegas. From this vantage point, the city unfolds like a lavish buffet, offering up all its delights in, theoretically, less than 20 minutes, no matter your choice of direction. It's here that Las Vegas reveals its surprisingly efficient side; a well-timed green light at these crossroads is like finding a $20 bill on the casino floor—an auspicious start to any journey.

Within the metro neighborhoods, a grid of wide arterial streets unfolds, making navigation relatively straightforward—if by straightforward, you mean occasionally confounding and often indirect. Plan for detours and back-ups, particularly near the Strip, where traffic can be as thick as the crowds at a blockbuster show.

Las Vegas Blvd South, better known as the Strip, is where driving can become a particularly hair-raising adventure. It's a stretch of road heavily frequented by tourists who seem more engrossed in the glittering marquees than road safety. Steering clear of distractions and allowing ample travel time are key here. Before long, newcomers adapt to the pace, dodging invigorated tourists and stressed locals with the agility of a seasoned Vegas performer.

Driving etiquette in Las Vegas can feel like navigating through a lively, ever-changing landscape, with experiences varying greatly from one person to the next. For some, the city's roads represent a bustling mix of speeds and styles, reflecting the diverse array of visitors and residents alike. There's a noted tendency for drivers to interpret speed limits with a wide range of enthusiasm, leading to an interesting dynamic on the freeways and streets. Weather conditions, especially rain, can quickly change the pace and rhythm of traffic, offering a reminder of nature's influence even in such a vibrant urban setting.

For the motorcycle riders out there: remember that in California, you can zip through traffic on your bike, but once you hit Nevada, that's a no-go, amigo! Vegas might be wild, but lane-splitting is a card you can't play here.

SUNGLASSES FOR YOUR CAR: TO TINT OR NOT TO TINT?

In the vibrant city of Las Vegas, deciding to tint your car windows is akin to choosing the perfect outfit for a night out on the Strip: it needs to be just right. Just as you wouldn't step out in attire that leaves you shivering or excessively warm, navigating the streets of this desert metropolis without the proper shading on your vehicle can lead to a similar discomfort—only, it's your car that's not appropriately dressed for the occasion.

Legal Regulations: Embarking on the tinting adventure? First up, remember that Vegas has its rules—not just for blackjack poker, but for your car's windows too. Keeping your tint within legal boundaries means smooth sailing ahead, without fines or unwanted stops. But beware, the legal limit might not give you the cloak of invisibility (or coolness) you desire, and stepping over the line could lead to a less than pleasant encounter with local law enforcement.

Heat Reduction: Tinting your car windows in Las Vegas isn't merely a matter of aesthetic preference or a bid for privacy from the curious gaze of fellow road travelers. It's a practical, almost indispensable strategy for coping with the relentless Nevada sun. The sun here doesn't just shine; it blazes with the intensity of a thousand stage lights, turning your car into a makeshift sauna if it's left unprotected. Just a heads up, though—not all tints are created equal, and some might fall short in the battle against the Vegas sun.

Cost: Adding a tint to your ride can range from a minor expense to a high-roller splurge. There are wallet-friendly options that keep you and your bank account cool. However, if you're eyeing the premium ceramic tints for their superior heat-blocking prowess, be prepared to pay top dollar, with prices that can reach up to $1,500 for the full monty.

Visibility: Good tinting can be like the perfect pair of sunglasses, reducing glare and enhancing your view of the road. But choose a tint that's too dark, and you might find night drives more thrilling than you bargained for, and not in a good way. Use common sense and know the legal limits, and you'll cruise right into that sweet spot between style and safety.

Privacy: In a city where privacy is as prized as a winning poker hand, a good tint can keep nosy onlookers at bay, letting you enjoy your ride in peace. Just remember, the quest for privacy with darker tints might draw unwanted attention from the law, turning your quest for solitude into a bit of a gamble.

AIRPORT: THE GATEWAY TO SIN CITY

Harry Reid International Airport (previously McCarran International Airport), just a stone's throw from the Strip, is the welcoming mat for visitors and locals alike. This bustling hub offers:

- Nonstop flights to a dizzying array of over 170 domestic and international destinations

- Quick connections to the Strip, Downtown, and the suburbs, with a journey time of just 20-30 minutes

- Over 1,700 daily departures and arrivals, making it as busy as a Vegas buffet line

- A logical Y-shaped terminal layout, ensuring you won't need breadcrumbs to find your way back from the baggage claim

- Convenient free cellphone lots and short-term parking for pickups

Harry Reid stands as a testament to Vegas's status as a world-class global transportation hub, consistently upgrading to meet the needs of the ever-growing number of visitors and locals.

ADVENTURES IN COMMUTING: A SURVIVAL GUIDE

Surviving, and dare we say thriving, in Las Vegas traffic demands a blend of wisdom, patience, and a dash of daring. Here are some tips to navigate the honking, bumper-to-bumper tide:

Timing is Everything: Much like betting on red or black, choose your travel times wisely. The early bird doesn't just catch the worm; it also avoids the snarl of traffic.

Knowledge is Power: Keeping an eye on traffic apps and local news can be the difference between a smooth cruise and a bumper-to-bumper grind. Forewarned is forearmed.

The Carpool Gambit: Employing the age-old strategy of carpooling can save time, money, and perhaps even the environment. Plus, it's a chance to make friends and allies in the daily battle against congestion—or at least have someone to vent to.

Embrace Alternatives: Occasionally, leaving the car at home and venturing forth via bus, monorail, or even on foot can transform a mundane commute into an opportunity for discovery.

EPILOGUE: NEON NAVIGATIONS

The journey from point A to B in Las Vegas is more than mere transit; it's a voyage through the heart of the city itself. From the strategic positioning of downtown living, offering a launchpad to every corner of the city, to the myriad transport options playing out like a hand of cards, navigating Las Vegas is an adventure in its own right. And so, armed with knowledge, insight, a bit of patience and a touch of humor, your transit through Las Vegas need not be a gamble, but a journey well worth the taking.

12. WATER WISDOM

In the heart of the desert, the importance of saving water takes on a whole new level of urgency. This isn't just about turning off the tap while brushing your teeth or fixing a leaky faucet, though those are commendable actions. It's about recognizing that in a city like Las Vegas, with its gleaming casinos and sprawling suburbs, every drop of water is as precious as a winning poker hand.

Las Vegas's reliance on the Colorado River is akin to a tightrope walker balancing precariously over a vast canyon. It's a fine line between abundance and crisis, and with the river under strain from overuse and drought, the stakes couldn't be higher. The city's desert setting, with its blistering heat and scarce rainfall, adds another layer of complexity to the water-saving equation. It's a place where the concept of water conservation takes on a nearly mythic importance, and is a critical mission in ensuring the oasis continues to thrive amidst the sands.

FLUSH WITH LIMITS: NAVIGATING LAS VEGAS'S WATER CONSERVATION POLICIES.

In Las Vegas, a set of water conservation policies have been rolled out to combat drought and make the most of the Colorado River's precious water. These strategies are designed to have a literal and figurative ripple effect through the community, impacting home owners in various ways.

Mandatory Watering Schedule: Residents and businesses are required to follow a mandatory watering schedule, which changes seasonally. This schedule dictates when irrigation systems may be operated, and there are penalties for non-compliance.

Grass Replacement Program: The Las Vegas Valley Water District encourages the removal of grass and its replacement with desert-friendly landscaping through a rebate program. This program pays residents to replace their turf with water-efficient landscaping, which can significantly reduce outdoor water use.

Water Waste Penalties: Penalties are imposed for water waste, such as allowing water to spray or flow off your property. This encourages residents to maintain their irrigation systems and avoid over-watering.

Limiting water usage: The Southern Nevada Water Authority (SNWA) has the power to limit water use for single-family residences that use more than half an acre-foot of water (approximately 163,000 gallons) per year. This measure targets the top 20% of water users and is designed to encourage conservation among those who consume the most water.

Public Education and Incentives: The SNWA provides resources and incentives for residents to conserve water, such as the Water Smart Landscapes rebate and the Tree Enhancement Program, which offers additional financial incentives for planting new trees.

WATER WHISPERS: SLY TIPS FOR THE THIRSTY HOME

Navigating the waters of conservation within the confines of one's abode, whether as a homeowner or a tenant, unfolds as a tale of ingenuity and determination.

The Quest for Modern Machinery: Imagine the gallant transformation from old to new as toilets, dishwashers, and washing machines evolve. The once water-guzzling beasts, devouring up to 6 gallons with a single gulp, are now replaced by efficient creatures that sip gently at the water, using a mere 1.28 gallons or less.

The Saga of the Dripping Faucet: Picture a realm where each drop from a leaky faucet joins forces with others, forming an invisible stream that could fill a small lake over time. Regular inspections and timely repairs in this domain can staunch the flow, keeping the water where it belongs.

Lifestyle Transformations: Simple acts, like turning off the tap while engaged in the daily rituals of teeth brushing or shaving, become acts of valor. Running the dishwasher and washing machine only when they're brimming with dishes and clothes transforms routine tasks into strategic moves in the great game of conservation.

The Enchantment of Water-Saving Fixtures: Installing fixtures labeled for their efficiency casts a spell of conservation across the land. Faucet aerators, once mundane, now serve as guardians of the realm, ensuring that every drop of water is used wisely.

The Chronicles of Watering by the Moon: By watering the land when the sun slumbers, one ensures that water reaches deep into the earth, nourishing the roots without a drop wasted to the heat of day or the breath of the wind.

The Masters of Moisture: Soaker hoses and drip irrigation systems deliver water directly to the earth's thirstiest inhabitants. Sprinklers, once wild and untamed, are now trained to avoid the folly of watering stone and pavement.

The Transformation of the Land: Envision a garden where the green sea of grass gives way to an eclectic tapestry of mulch, ground cover, and drought-resistant plants. Here, beauty thrives with but a fraction of the water once demanded by their thirstier ancestors.

Harvesters of the Sky: Capturing rainwater is akin to bottling the sky's bounty, a resource saved for the drier days. This ancient practice renews the bond between sky and earth, providing life-sustaining moisture to the garden with the turn of a spigot.

The Noble Car Wash: When the chariot requires cleansing, seek out the sanctuaries where water is recycled, or embrace the simplicity of a bucket and sponge. Such acts, though small, ripple through the fabric of conservation, sustaining the precious resource that is water.

VEGAS WATER: A HARD BET

Let's take a detour from water conservation, to explore a topic that might not make the headlines but certainly affects the daily lives of its residents and visitors alike: the city's notably hard water. According to a report by Homewater 101, Las Vegas has the distinction of having the second hardest water in the entire nation. Now, for those unacquainted with the term, "hard water" isn't a reference to ice or anything frozen, but rather to water that's rich in dissolved minerals, particularly calcium and magnesium.

Imagine turning on your tap in the Las Vegas Valley and finding out that the water flowing out has a hardness level of 278 parts per million, or 16 grains per gallon. It's a scenario where the terms "very hard" and "extremely hard" are not just descriptors but lived realities for the residents. This high mineral content can turn simple daily tasks, like lathering soap or washing dishes, into a chore, leaving behind a telltale residue on everything from your shower doors to your favorite glassware.

The battle against hard water in Las Vegas is not unique but emblematic of a broader issue affecting 85 percent of the United States. The culprit? The city's primary water source, Lake Mead, which is fed by the mineral-laden Colorado River. This geological and hydrological cocktail results in water that's laden with minerals.

If you hail from a state that flows with soft or moderately hard water, you'll notice a difference in taste. But despite its hardness, the water in Las Vegas is still perfectly safe to drink, meeting or exceeding all federal Safe Drinking Water Act standards. It's a testament to the city's resilience and its ability to provide for its inhabitants, even in the face of challenging natural conditions.

The presence of hard water has led to a proliferation of household solutions, from rinse aids for your dishwasher to specially formulated laundry detergents, all designed to mitigate the effects of those extra minerals. It's a small but constant reminder of the unique challenges faced by those living in and visiting Las Vegas, a city better known for its entertainment and nightlife than for the hardness quotient of its water supply.

Yet, this issue adds another layer to the complex identity of Las Vegas, a city that continually adapts to and overcomes its environmental challenges. It's a reminder that behind the iconic glamour of the city, the residents are navigating everyday issues, like hard water, that connect them to broader environmental and geological phenomena. In the end, the story of Las Vegas's hard water is a slice of life in this vibrant city, reflecting its indomitable spirit and the practical realities of desert living.

EPILOGUE: CONSERVATION OR BUST

The city of Las Vegas stands at a crucial juncture. The efforts toward water conservation, though occasionally inconvenient, are vital for sustaining this vibrant oasis. These measures, from mandatory watering schedules to incentives for water-efficient landscaping, may sometimes be a nuisance—but they are essential.

And the resilience and creativity of Las Vegas's residents in facing these challenges highlight a collective commitment to preserving every precious drop of water. This journey, while demanding small sacrifices, is a necessary step to ensure the future prosperity of the city amidst the arid landscape. It's a testament to the fact that in Las Vegas, the spirit of innovation and community is the true wellspring that never runs dry.

13.   ENTERTAINMENT AND LEISURE

Beneath its more famous qualities, such as its nighttime neon glow and the incessant ding-ding-ding of slot machines, Las Vegas is a wealth of additional cultural and recreational experiences that are as varied and intriguing as the stories that echo down its Strip. It's a world where the juxtaposition of urban exuberance against the stark, natural beauty of Nevada's landscape creates a playground for every ilk of adventurer.

CULTURAL OASIS

Artistic Alleys and Havens: Las Vegas's Arts District, known affectionately as "18b," is the beating heart of the city's creative community. Wander through streets brimming with galleries, boutiques, and murals that transform the area into a living canvas. The monthly First Friday event turns the district into a celebratory amalgamation of art, music, and culinary delights.

The Smith Center for the Performing Arts: This five-acre, three-theater, located in Downtown Las Vegas' Symphony Park hosts everything from Broadway tours to concerts and performances by the Las Vegas Philharmonic. It's a cultural feast, and not the kind you'd expect in a city known for its expansive buffet offerings.

The Historical Underpinnings: For those intrigued by the less glitzy, more gritty history of Las Vegas, the Neon Museum features a collection of the city's iconic, evocative neon signs, each with its own storied past. Meanwhile, the Mob Museum delves into the entangled history of organized crime and law enforcement in the city, an interactive testament to Las Vegas's fraught and checkered beginnings.

The Sphere: This ultra-modern marvel, resembling a giant's marble, is the new hotspot for an eclectic mix of events, ranging from avant-garde concerts to dynamic corporate gatherings and flashy product unveilings. Step inside, and you'll find yourself wrapped in a cocoon of cutting-edge LED screens, enveloping half the Sphere's interior, dazzling spectators with visuals that make the performances especially vivid.

Bellagio Gallery of Fine Art (BGFA): Situated within the Bellagio Hotel, this gallery hosts world-class art exhibitions from both international and domestic scenes. The rotating exhibits ensure that visitors always have something new and intriguing to explore, making it a popular tourist destination and a staple for the local art lovers.

A Vegas Show: And of course, the nightly Cirque du Soleil shows and residencies by superstars like Adele and Sting add just the right amount of glitz to the cultural mix.

RECREATIONAL ESCAPADES OUTDOORS

Las Vegas' enviable weather is a jackpot for anyone who loves the great outdoors. Year-round adventures await in the surrounding desert ecosystem, which, by the way, is far more than just a vast expanse of sand.

Hiking Beyond the Neon: Red Rock Canyon dazzles with panoramic views, trails that range from leisurely walks to challenging hikes, and rock climbing routes that offer an upward adventure. Similarly, the Valley of Fire State Park, with its ancient petroglyphs and stunning red sandstone formations, provides a colorful escape into Nevada's ancient landscapes. Sloan Canyon is a bit less crowded than some of the other areas mentioned, but is equally rich in natural beauty and cultural history. Tule Springs Fossil Beds National Monument is a relatively new addition to the National Park System, protecting Ice Age fossils and providing a fascinating glimpse into the ancient past of the Las Vegas Valley.

A Lake in the Desert: Lake Mead National Recreation Area offers a watery reprieve from the desert's embrace. Boating, fishing, and swimming in the reservoir's cool blues provide a perfect antidote both to the hustle and bustle of the as well as the sun's relentless rays.

Winter Wonderland: For the snow bunnies among us, Mt. Charleston Ski Resort is just 45 minutes from downtown and offers downhill skiing and snowboarding. It's a wonderland that feels worlds away from the neon and noise of the city.

Natural Hot Tub: For those willing to take on a challenging hike, Gold Strike Hot Springs offers a series of hot spring pools nestled in a dramatic canyon. It's a rewarding adventure for experienced hikers, especially during cooler weather.

Camping and Stargazing: Valley of Fire State Park is a must-visit. With its petrified logs and ancient petroglyphs, it's like stepping back in time. The state park around Vegas offers gateways to other worlds, each with their own unique charm and character, demonstrating Vegas' impressive geological marvels and range of outdoor pursuits.

FAMILY ADVENTURES IN THE CITY

Las Vegas shines as a family-friendly destination with myriad attractions designed to delight both the younger crowd and the young at heart.

Interactive Museums & Exhibits:

- The Discovery Children's Museum, with its three stories of interactive exhibits, nurtures curiosity and learning through play.

- The Shark Reef Aquarium at Mandalay Bay provides an underwater journey through a predator-filled shipwreck.

- Las Vegas Natural History Museum offers an extensive range of exhibits that cover topics from prehistoric life and dinosaurs to Egyptian artifacts and marine life.

- Springs Preserve is a cultural institution designed to commemorate Las Vegas's dynamic history and provide a vision for a sustainable future. It features botanical gardens, walking trails, interactive exhibits, and live animal shows, making it an excellent place for families to learn about the desert environment.

Adrenaline-Fueled Fun:

- Adventuredome, an indoor amusement park at Circus Circus, offers thrill rides, mini-golf, and laser tag—a universe of fun under a pink glass dome.

- For go-kart enthusiasts, tracks like Gene Woods Racing Experience offer high-speed fun and excitement.

- The STRAT Tower caters to thrill-seekers with a lineup of heart-pounding rides. Get launched skyward on Big Shot, teeter over the edge on X-Scream, or spin at dizzying speeds on Insanity The Ride. For the ultimate rush, take the plunge with SkyJump Las Vegas, a controlled descent from 829 feet— but don't forget to check restrictions before braving these adrenaline-pumping adventures. An age-requirement of 14 or above applies, for example.

- For families looking to cool off from the desert heat, Cowabunga Bay offers a fun-filled day with water slides, a wave pool, and a lazy river. It's a seasonal attraction that provides a refreshing escape during the warmer months.

Multiverse of Entertainment:

- Round 1: Whether you're channeling your inner Kingpin on the polished lanes or battling for arcade supremacy, Round 1 provides a vibrant arena for relaxation and friendly competition. www.round1usa.com
- AREA15: An immersive entertainment and retail complex that blends art, technology, and design to create unique experiences such as interactive installations, events, and exhibits that push the boundaries of traditional entertainment, making it a modern cultural institution in its own right.

Free Family Gems

- Ethel M Chocolate Factory and Botanical Cactus Garden: For a sweet adventure, families can tour the Ethel M Chocolate Factory to see how chocolates are made and then wander through the adjacent Botanical Cactus Garden, one of the world's largest collections of its kind. The factory tour is free, and visitors often get a complimentary sample of chocolate.
- If your family enjoys nature, the Henderson Bird Viewing Preserve offers paths that wind through nine ponds set aside for birdwatching. It's a peaceful place to see a variety of birds and other wildlife. Entry is free, and it's a wonderful way to spend a morning or afternoon.

- One of the largest parks in Las Vegas, Sunset Park offers plenty of picnic areas, ponds for fishing, walking trails, and open space for kids to run around. It's a great spot for a family day out.

THE ALLURE OF LOCAL LIFE

Springs Preserve: In a city synonymous with human-made spectacles, the Springs Preserve offers a refreshing counterpoint, a sanctuary dedicated to the natural wonders of the Mojave Desert. This cultural institution turned botanical garden provides a green haven where locals and visitors alike can immerse themselves in the region's rich ecological and historical tapestry. With trails meandering through vibrant desert landscapes, museums that chronicle the valley's past, and galleries that ignite the imagination, the Springs Preserve encapsulates the multifaceted beauty of Nevada's natural heritage. www.springspreserve.org

Community Gatherings: Farmers' markets like the Fresh52 Farmers' & Artisan Market provide a taste of local life, offering fresh produce, handmade goods, and a chance to mingle with other market enthusiasts.

A Green Respite: For moments of tranquility, Floyd Lamb Park is a verdant oasis set against the backdrop of Tule Springs, offering picnicking, fishing, and peacocks that roam with an air of royalty.

A MEDLEY OF COMMUNITY FESTIVALS

In the effervescent city of Las Vegas, community events and festivals are not just happenings, they are grand celebrations of life, threads in the vibrant tapestry of Las Vegas culture, offering both locals and wanderers from afar a splendid chance to delve into the city's diverse interests and rich heritage.

Las Vegas Book Festival: The largest literary event in Nevada, this festival is a celebration of literature's magic. Attracting both local and national authors, it's a bibliophile's dream come true—a meeting ground for book lovers, featuring author readings, book signings, panel discussions, and workshops.

Age of Chivalry Renaissance Festival: Held at Sunset Park, this festival is a delightful throwback to the Renaissance period. It offers a chance to experience the era's traditions with knights, jesters, and a market of artisanal crafts. It's a historical escapade right in the heart of modern Vegas.

Life is Beautiful Festival: This festival transforms Downtown Las Vegas into a canvas of cultural celebration. It's a unique blend of music, art, and food, showcasing top musical acts and artists. The festival is a testament to Las Vegas's vibrant contemporary arts scene.

Las Vegas Pride: Celebrating the LGBTQ+ community, Las Vegas Pride is a colorful, inclusive event. It includes a parade and a festival with live entertainment, highlighting the city's commitment to diversity and inclusivity.

Super Summer Theatre: At Spring Mountain Ranch State Park, this outdoor theatre series is a summer highlight. It provides family-friendly entertainment with Broadway-style performances under the stars, combining natural beauty with theatrical charm.

The Great Vegas Festival of Beer: A celebration of the craft beer culture, this festival features an extensive selection of beers from across the globe. With tastings, food pairings, and music, it's a favorite for beer lovers.

EPILOGUE: BEYOND THE NEON

Dive beyond Las Vegas's gleaming facade to discover a world brimming with culture, nature, and endless adventure. From the creative pulse of the Arts District to the natural wonders that frame the city, Vegas offers myriad, unique experiences far richer than any casino jackpot. It's a city where every corner promises discovery and every moment can be an unforgettable adventure. Welcome to the vibrant heart of Las Vegas, where the real magic awaits beyond the expected.

14.   DINING AND SHOPPING

Las Vegas, a city where the dazzling and the opulent are as common as daylight in the desert, is home to an embarrassment of riches when it comes to dining and shopping. Here, amidst the labyrinth of lights, slot machines, and poker tables, lie culinary jewels and retail havens begging to be discovered by the intrepid explorer.

A GASTRONOMIC ODYSSEY

Las Vegas's restaurant scene is as varied and vibrant as the city itself, with a melting pot of global cuisines—each eatery offering a portal to a different part of the globe or even another time in history.

My personal culinary journey in Vegas began with a challenge I called "The World Tour Buffet Challenge." Every day I sampled cuisine from all over the world at a different buffet. On day one, I indulged in pasta, on day two I discovered dim sum. By day four, I was a mix of excitement and indigestion, questioning the wisdom of my challenge. In a lavish seafood buffet on day four, I reached my limit. After sitting there for a few minutes, surrounded by half-eaten plates of global delicacies, I realized Vegas dining isn't just about quantity; it's also about quality and variety. The challenge turned into a lesson for about the city's culinary diversity—and my own self discipline. From then on, I chose to savor every culinary experience, one meal at a time.

FOR THE STAR-STRUCK GOURMAND:

Restaurant Guy Savoy: $$$ Prepare for a symphony of foie gras, truffles, and caviar at this Strip stalwart. Michelin-starred Chef Savoy reigns supreme, crafting French haute cuisine that's as dazzling as the Bellagio fountains. Be prepared to splurge, but savor every bite of this culinary achievement. (702) 731-7286

Jaleo by José Andrés: $$$ Craving a fiesta for the senses? This vibrant ode to Spanish tapas by culinary rockstar José Andrés is the answer. From sizzling *gambas al ajillo* to melt-in-your-mouth *jamón ibérico*, Jaleo's tapas parade will leave you humming flamenco music and plotting your next visit. (702) 698-7950

Gordon Ramsay Hell's Kitchen: $$$ Located at Caesars Palace, this restaurant brings to life the TV show's setting, featuring dishes from the famous (and famously acerbic) chef Gordon Ramsay. It's a hotspot for fans of the show and those who appreciate fine British cuisine with a modern twist. (702) 731-7373

L'Atelier: $$$ This is a luxurious dining experience offering exquisite French cuisine by the late chef Joël Robuchon. Located in the MGM Grand, it's known for its opulent setting and impeccable service, making it a must-visit for those seeking a lavish dining experience. (702) 891-7358

Momofuku: $$ Created by the renowned chef David Chang, Momofuku at The Cosmopolitan offers an innovative menu that combines elements of Korean, Japanese, and American cuisines. It's known for its creative dishes and vibrant atmosphere. (702) 698-2663

Bazaar Meat by José Andrés: $$$ Another creation of José Andrés, Bazaar Meat in the Sahara Las Vegas is a celebration of all things carnivorous, offering a unique and adventurous take on the steakhouse concept. (702) 761-7610

Nobu: $$$ Located inside Caesars Palace, Nobu is a world-renowned Japanese restaurant offering an exquisite array of sushi and other Japanese dishes, crafted by the acclaimed chef Nobu Matsuhisa. (702) 785-6628

FOR THE ADVENTUROUS PALATE:

Pier 88 Boiling Seafood & Bar: $$ Ditch the buffets, grab a bib, and get ready to get messy! Pier 88 isn't your average Vegas joint. Think steaming cauldrons overflowing with Cajun crawfish, plump shrimp, and snow crab legs—a flavor fiesta that'll have you saying *"laissez les bon temps rouler!"* (That's "Let the good times roll!" in Louisiana French, *cher.*) Plastic gloves and communal tables set the scene for an unforgettable, hands-on seafood adventure. www.pier88seafood.com

Le Thai: $$ A vibrant spot in downtown Las Vegas known for its flavorful and authentic Thai cuisine. Diners can explore an array of spicy dishes, traditional curries, and unique flavors that are sure to tantalize the taste buds of adventurous eaters. (702) 778-0888

Lotus of Siam: $$$ Widely acclaimed for its Northern Thai cuisine, Lotus of Siam presents a range of unique dishes that go beyond the usual Thai menu. With its emphasis on complex flavors and spices, it's a must-visit for those looking to explore Thai cuisine in depth. Phone: (702) 735-3033.

Raku: $$$ This Japanese grill in Chinatown is known for its authentic and creative approach to robatayaki and izakaya-style dining. Raku's menu features a variety of grilled skewers, unique small plates, and adventurous options like grilled offal. (702) 367-3511.

Hot N Juicy Crawfish: $$ Roll up your sleeves and dive into a spicy, hands-on experience with seafood. This place is all about flavorful, boil-in-bag seafood with a choice of seasonings and heat levels, perfect for those who love a tactile and tasty adventure. (702) 891-8889.

Marrakech Moroccan Restaurant: $$$ This immersive restaurant offers not just a meal, but an experience with belly dancing, vibrant decor, and a six-course Moroccan feast served in traditional style. The flavors and atmosphere here are truly an adventure for the senses. (702) 737-5611.

Blackout—Dining in the Dark: $$$ For a truly unique experience, Blackout offers a meal in complete darkness, heightening your other senses. The menu is a surprise (not that you'd be able to see it, anyway), adding to the adventurous and unpredictable nature of a dining experience like no other. dineblackout.com

FOR THE BUDGET-CONSCIOUS BON VIVANT:

Tacos El Gordo: $ Forget fancy tablecloths, this is taco nirvana on a paper plate. Pile your tortillas with succulent barbacoa, melt-in-your-mouth carnitas, and juicy al pastor, all for a song. Lines snaking around the block are a testament to their legendary status—so grab a cold *agua fresca* and savor the anticipation. (702) 476-0684

Metro Pizza: $ Vegas has a burgeoning "secret slice" scene, and Metro Pizza is its reigning champion. Forget cardboard delivery slices—here, wood-fired pies with chewy crusts and tangy tomato sauce emerge from a roaring oven, ready to fill your wallet and your stomach for under $15. metropizza.com

Lou's Diner: $ Step into a time warp at Lou's, where the vibe is vintage and the breakfasts are legendary. Imagine fluffy pancakes, eggs cooked just right, and bacon that's the perfect level of crispy— all served with a side of nostalgia. Lou's is where the locals flock for a taste of classic Americana. It's comfort food heaven, dished out with a smile and a price that's as friendly as the service. (702) 870-1876

Sakana Sushi: $$ Dive into a sea of sushi without breaking the bank at Sakana Sushi, where Tokyo meets Vegas in an all-you-can-eat extravaganza! This gem offers more than just sushi; it's a wallet-friendly feast with a side of artistic flair. Imagine endless rounds of perfectly sliced sashimi, creatively rolled sushi, and nigiri that's as easy on the wallet as it is on the palate. With a cozy setting and inviting ambiance, Sakana is the go-to spot for both sushi aficionados and casual diners alike. (725) 258-6684

In-N-Out Burger: $ For those moving to Las Vegas from the California, In-N-Out Burger might be a familiar delight, but it's an absolute must-try for uninitiated visitors from areas such as New York that don't offer access to the unique experience that many East Coasters ultimately find superior even to Shake Shack (gasp!). In-N-Out is renowned for its simple yet exceptionally tasty menu. It's a staple of West Coast fast food culture, and a delightful discovery for those who haven't had the pleasure yet.

THE RETAIL REALM

Shopping in Las Vegas is akin to setting sail in a sea of endless choices, from high-end boutiques that adorn the Strip to quirky shops that dot its lesser-known quarters.

FOR THE VINTAGE HUNTER:

Patina Décor: Famous for its eclectic mix of vintage furniture, charming home decorations, trendy lighting, and retro fashion, the store is a treasure trove for anyone hunting for one-of-a-kind, stylish vintage finds. It's the go-to spot for locals and tourists alike who want to sprinkle their homes or closets with items that are not just unique but also steeped in history. Just a heads up though—the prices aren't exactly thrift store bargains! 1300 S Main St ste 140, Las Vegas, NV 89104, (702)-776-6222

Vintage Vegas Antiques: Ditch the Strip, and dive into this trip! Vintage Vegas serves up retro radness, from casino relics to quirky finds. It's no ordinary antique shop—think "old stuff *and* cool crap." Neon signs blaze, staff guides your time travel, and every purchase whispers tales of poodle skirts and martinis. Get your nostalgia fix, Vegas style! 1229 S Main St, Las Vegas, NV 89104, (702) 539-0799

Antique Alley: Step back in time and embark on a treasure hunt at Antique Alley. This charming enclave of over 65 independent vendors, located on Main Street just north of the Stratosphere, boasts a vibrant collection of antiques, collectibles, vintage clothing, furniture, and art. From Victorian porcelain to mid-century modern furniture, prepare to unearth unique finds and bargain with passionate collectors. 1126 S Main St, Las Vegas, NV 89104, (702) 684-5177

Charleston Antique Mall: This sprawling haven (an impressive 18,000 square feet!) tells its stories of yesteryear via vintage finds galore. Imagine: mid-century magic, chrome-kissed lamps, and quirky trinkets—a treasure trove for your inner antique enthusiast. Over 60 seasoned dealers showcase their finds, offering something that will grant every collector's wish. 560 S. Decatur Blvd., Las Vegas, NV 89107, (702) 228-4783

Buffalo Exchange: Known for its selection of vintage T-shirts and fashion-forward second-hand clothing, Buffalo Exchange is a favorite among those looking for curated collections. While prices may be higher due to the fashion focus, many find the cost reasonable for the quality and uniqueness of items. 1209 S Main St, Las Vegas, NV 89104, (702) 791-3960

Castaways: Located on Stephanie Promenade, Castaways stands out not just for its unbeatable prices, offering budget-conscious consumers a treasure trove of low-cost casual wear and home furnishings, but also for its remarkable social mission. The store leverages the repurposed industry to empower former inmates, providing them with opportunities to rebuild their lives and support their families. 241 N Stephanie St, Henderson, NV 89074, (702) 425-9146

Deseret Industries: This store is highly regarded for its extensive selection of furniture, video games, and collectibles, offering exceptional deals across a diverse range of products. With its wide array of goods available at competitive prices, the store has become a favored destination for bargain hunters and those in search of budget-friendly shopping options. 3750 West Craig Road, North Las Vegas, Nevada 89032, (702) 649-8191

FOR THE BARGAINISTA:

Fremont Street Experience: Not a bargain destination per se, but you'll find a treasure trove of unique shops at Fremont Street Experience. Score quirky souvenirs, handcrafted jewelry, and vintage finds amidst the electrifying buzz of Downtown. Fremont St E between Main St & I-95, Las Vegas, NV 89101

Las Vegas North Premium Outlets: Escape the Strip and head north for even deeper discounts at the Las Vegas North Premium Outlets. Score deals on brands like Michael Kors, Coach, and Nike, all nestled amidst lush landscaping and a relaxed atmosphere. 8700 Las Vegas Blvd N, Las Vegas, NV 89115, (702) 252-1200

Las Vegas South Premium Outlets: Venture south from the Strip to discover unbeatable bargains at the Las Vegas South Premium Outlets. Find exceptional savings on luxury and leading brands such as Michael Kors, Coach, Movado, and Polo Ralph Lauren all set within a picturesque shopping environment that promises a pleasant and leisurely shopping experience. 7400 Las Vegas Blvd S, Las Vegas, NV 89123, (702) 896-5599

Macy's Backstage: Within Macy's department stores, Macy's Backstage offers a unique treasure hunt with its off-price shopping experience. Discover great finds on clothing, home decor, cosmetics, and more at discounted prices, adding an exciting twist to conventional department store shopping. 4300 Meadows Lane, Las Vegas, NV 89107, (702) 880-6601

REGIONAL FLAIR:

Las Vegas, with its diverse cultures and one-of-a-kind experiences, is home to a unique blend of regional chains that offer locals and visitors alike a taste of the world. From electronics and home goods designed for the culturally savvy shopper to grocery stores that bring the flavors of Latin America and Asia right to your doorstep, these chains make up a surprisingly special part of Las Vegas's retail landscape.

Curacao: This chain offering a wide range of electronics, home furnishings, and appliances, along with services like travel arrangements and finance options. Curacao stores are designed to provide a culturally relevant shopping experience.

Cardenas Markets: Specializing in Latin American groceries, Cardenas Markets offer a variety of fresh produce, meats, seafood, and bakery items, along with an array of imported goods from Latin American countries. Shoppers can find authentic flavors and traditional ingredients not commonly carried by mainstream supermarkets.

99 Ranch Market: While 99 Ranch Market has started to expand beyond the Southwest, its presence in Las Vegas offers a vast selection of Asian groceries, including fresh produce, seafood, and an array of Asian food products that might be harder to find in typical markets.

EōS Fitness: While New York has its share of gym chains, EōS Fitness is a rapidly growing fitness center chain in the Southwest, including several locations in Las Vegas. It's known for its affordable memberships, wide range of equipment and fitness classes, catering to both casual gym-goers and fitness enthusiasts.

El Super: A supermarket chain that focuses on offering a wide range of Mexican and Latin American grocery items, including fresh produce, meats, and bakery items. El Super is known for its competitive prices and a large selection of items that cater to the tastes and preferences of the Hispanic community.

FOR THE VARIETY SEEKER:

Meadows Mall: Beyond outlet deals and Strip glamor, the Meadows Mall offers a convenient, family-friendly shopping experience. Browse department stores like Dillard's and JCPenney or grab a bite at Auntie Anne's. The Meadows Mall provides a one-stop shop for everyday needs and casual browsing. 4300 Meadows Ln, Las Vegas, NV 89124, (702) 456-877

Fashion Show Las Vegas: As the largest shopping, dining, and entertainment destination on the Las Vegas Strip, Fashion Show Las Vegas boasts over 250 retailers and more than 30 restaurants across 2 million square feet. It features anchor stores such as Neiman Marcus, Forever 21, Nordstrom, and Saks Fifth Avenue, alongside a variety of dining options including The Capital Grille and El Segundo Sol. 3200 Las Vegas Blvd. S., Las Vegas, NV 89109

Downtown Summerlin Shopping Centre: This open-air, pet-friendly shopping complex is one of the newest additions to Las Vegas's shopping scene. It offers a mix of shops and restaurants, including Dillard's, Macy's, Forever21, and dining options like Wolfgang Puck's Bar and Grill. Location: 1980 Festival Plaza Dr., Las Vegas, NV 89135

Town Square Las Vegas: One-of-a-kind retail, dining, and entertainment destination features 26 architecturally distinctive buildings, public parks, and water features. It's a premiere spot for shopping, dining, and entertainment, offering extended hours for restaurants and bars. Las Vegas Boulevard at the junction of I-15 and the 215 Beltway

SAVORING AND SHOPPING WITH SENSIBILITY

Navigating Las Vegas's dining and shopping landscape requires a blend of adventurous spirit and sage sensibility. Here are a few tips to enhance the journey:

Reserve Ahead: For top dining spots, making reservations is as crucial as holding the winning hand. A bit of foresight ensures a seat at the culinary table of your choice.

Exploration Pays: Venturing beyond the well-trod tourist paths can uncover dining delights and shopping steals that provide a more authentic and often more memorable Vegas experience.

Timing is Key: Shopping during off-peak hours avoids the crowds, making the hunt for that perfect piece or deal a more leisurely affair. Similarly, dining during off-peak times can lead to more attentive service and a relaxed atmosphere.

Loyalty Rewards: Many Vegas establishments offer loyalty programs that reward frequent visitors with discounts, special offers, and other perks. Signing up can transform a regular night out into an exclusive experience.

Happy Hour Hunting: Many top-tier restaurants and bars in Vegas boast happy hour specials, presenting an opportunity to sample gourmet bites and craft cocktails at a fraction of the regular price.

EPILOGUE: FAREWELL FEAST

As we conclude our tour of Las Vegas's culinary wonders and shopping sprees, we carry with us mouth-watering memories from this city of endless dazzle and surprise. In this city, dining is not merely eating, and shopping transcends mere purchasing. It's about embracing an adventure that reveals the heart of Vegas—one plate and one purchase at a time.

As we fold the map of our Las Vegas adventure, we realize that the real treasures were the experiences gathered along the way—each meal savored, each unique find, a story to hold. Vegas, in its grandeur and mystery, invites us to explore, taste, and treasure every moment.

15.   COMMUNITY AND SOCIAL LIFE

Moving to Las Vegas—a city known for its brilliant lights, bustling casinos, and a strong undercurrent of communal warmth—can be as daunting as trying to find a slot machine that actually pays out. Yet, beneath its glittering surface, Las Vegas is teeming with opportunities to find your tribe and engage with social circles that can transform the city from a place you moved to, into a place you call home.

THE ART OF COMMUNITY FORGING

Las Vegas may have its fair share of visitors, but it is also home to burgeoning and long-standing communities, each offering a unique blend of interests, activities, and, most importantly, camaraderie. Finding these groups, however, requires a dash of adventurous spirit and a pinch of good old-fashioned sleuthing.

The Usual (and Not So Usual) Suspects: Sure, one could argue that joining a gym, attending a religious institution, or volunteering are standard fare for those looking to knit themselves into the fabric of a new city, but in Las Vegas offers its own fresh take—as it does with almost everything else.

DIGITAL DIVING BOARDS INTO THE SOCIAL POOL

In an age where our lives are as digital as they are physical, platforms like Meetup and Facebook Groups serve as modern-day town squares, bustling with activity and ripe with opportunity for social connection.

Meetup (www.meetup.com): A treasure trove of Las Vegas-based groups can be unearthed here, ranging from hiking enthusiasts and book clubs to tech meetups and board game nights. This digital arena is where interests of all shades find their communal spirit.

Facebook Groups: Search for Las Vegas in the Groups section, and you'll be met with a multitude of communities. Whether you're passionate about photography, baking, or sustainable living, there's likely a group waiting for you to hit 'Join.'

Reddit: Venture over to Reddit and explore subreddits like r/vegaslocals, r/movingtovegas and r/VegasJobs. These communities offer a blend of local news, social gatherings, discussions about life in Las Vegas, and job opportunities. Subreddits like r/lasvegashiking could also pique the interest of outdoor enthusiasts.

EVENTS AND HAPPENINGS: THE CITY'S PULSE

Las Vegas, ever the host, is abundant in events that cater to nearly every interest under the sun (or neon light, in this case).

First Friday: An art-centric celebration that transforms the streets of downtown's Arts District into a canvas of creativity, food, and music. It's where art lovers and the culturally curious converge, offering a perfect backdrop for serendipitous encounters and the weaving of social threads.

Farmers Markets: The Las Vegas Farmers Market (with locations listed at www.lasvegasfarmersmarket.com) and others dot the cityscape, providing not just fresh produce but fresh conversations, serving as wholesome venues to meet health-minded individuals and taste the local flavor—literally and metaphorically.

The Writer's Block: This independent bookstore buzzes with the excitement of author events, where words leap off the page and into lively discussions. It's a place where book clubs convene, turning the

turning   of   pages   into   a   communal   celebration.
www.thewritersblock.org

The Avantpop Bookstore: This is not your grandma's bookstore—well, it is if she's into counterculture, dabbling in the occult, supporting BIPOC voices, and swooning over romance novels—and why not? This indie gem doubles as a publisher and is a go-to spot for any-aged adult for events and workshops that are as unique as the books on its shelves. www.avantpopbooks.com/home

The libraries: Clark County libraries are where adults can attend to their inner bookworm, tech guru, or secret artist (kids can too, but in junior form). With a lineup that includes everything from artsy afternoons and book clubs to creative writing workshops and tech tutorials. events.thelibrarydistrict.org/events?r=thismonth

TheList.Vegas: your handpicked ticket to Las Vegas's most dazzling cultural happenings, where the city's arts scene comes alive in a curated showcase of pure entertainment and flair. thelist.vegas

VOLUNTEERING: THE ALTRUISTIC NETWORK

For those drawn to making a meaningful impact within their community, volunteering emerges as more than a noble endeavor—it's a golden chance to forge impactful connections.

Diving into the world of volunteering in Las Vegas is as easy as visiting these organizations' websites or giving them a ring. Whether you're a conservationist, mentor, advocate, animal lover, or someone open to making a difference, there's a slot in the Las Vegas volunteer scene just waiting for your token of time. It's an opportunity to hit the jackpot of fulfillment, community, and purpose, proving that what happens in Vegas doesn't just stay in Vegas—it changes lives.

Environmental Conservation and Outdoor Activities: For those with a green thumb or an adventurous spirit, the Nevada Wilderness Project (www.nevadawilderness.org/volunteer) beckons with the promise of conservation efforts that are as rewarding as they are rigorous. Think of it as your gym membership for the soul. Similarly, Get Outdoors Nevada (getoutdoorsnevada.org/get-involved/volunteer-opportunities/) offers a lighter fare of outdoor conservation activities—perfect for dipping your toes into Mother Nature's waters.

Supporting Children and Education: If you've ever fancied yourself a mentor or an educator, organizations like Big Brothers Big Sisters (www.bbbsn.org/become-a-big) and Green Our Planet (www.greenourplanet.org) are ready to enroll you in the rewarding school of shaping young minds. From mentoring to teaching kids the ABCs of agriculture, it's a chance to grow futures (and maybe even some vegetables along the way).

Helping the Homeless and Underserved Communities: For those who find fulfillment in lending a hand to those in need, the Las Vegas Rescue Mission (www.vegasrescue.org/volunteer/) and Catholic Charities of Southern Nevada (www.catholiccharities.com/get-involved/volunteer) are like the buffet of volunteerism—offering a variety of ways to serve, from kitchen duty to thrift store chic. Project 150 (https://www.project150.org/volunteer-with-us) helps homeless teens with essentials, from food to education—because sometimes, the biggest heroes are the ones who offer a helping hand.

Animal Welfare: Animal enthusiasts can unleash their passion with Hearts Alive Village (www.heartsalivevillage.org/volunteer/) or the SPCA (https://nevadaspca.org/volunteer/), where caring for furry friends offers a purr-fect blend of joy and fulfillment. It's like being a superhero, with a cape that is perpetually covered in pet hair.

Feeding the Community: Organizations like Three Square (www.threesquare.org), Southern Nevada's largest food bank, serve up more than just meals; they dish out avenues to give back, meet kindred spirits, and embed your Las Vegas journey with a sense of shared purpose. Volunteering here is less about culinary skills and more about stirring up hope, one packed meal at a time.

Miscellaneous Volunteer Opportunities: For those looking for a unique twist to their volunteer experience, Opportunity Village (www.opportunityvillage.org/get-involved/volunteer) serves people with intellectual and related disabilities. The Cupcake Girls (www.thecupcakegirls.org/) sweeten the deal by supporting survivors of sex trafficking, providing an act of kindness with every sprinkle. The Shade Tree (theshadetree.org/volunteer/) offers a special blend of shelter and life-changing services to abused women and women with children in crisis, proving that compassion is the most powerful force of all.

FANTASY AND FANDOM: HOTSPOTS FOR GEEKING OUT

Las Vegas, a city famed for its electrifying nightlife and casino buzz, also boasts a treasure trove of spots perfect for nerds and superfans. Beyond the glittering Strip, there exists a vibrant community where like-minded individuals can connect over shared hobbies and interests. From cozy board game cafes to lively theme bars, Las Vegas offers numerous venues where newcomers to the city can meet others who share their passions. Here's a guide to the top places in Las Vegas for nerds to hang out and meet fellow enthusiasts, especially if you've recently moved to town.

Knight & Day Games: A haven for Dungeons & Dragons fans, Knight & Day Games is located in Town Square and is renowned for its D&D sessions every Sunday at 11 am. This spot is celebrated for its welcoming environment to players of all levels, including novices eager to embark on their first quest. The Dungeon Master's enthusiasm for teaching new players makes Knight & Day Games an ideal location for newcomers to Las Vegas looking to join a community of tabletop RPG enthusiasts. knightanddaygames.com

Millennium Fandom Bar: Millennium Fandom Bar is a theme bar that stands as a social hub for individuals looking to connect over shared interests in the perfect setting. Famous for its themed nights, the bar offers a welcoming space for fans of various fandoms. Whether you're into sci-fi, fantasy, or comic books, Millennium provides a lively atmosphere where new residents can easily strike up conversations and form lasting friendships with like-minded locals. fandombar.com

Meepleville Board Game Café: Boasting an extensive library of board games, Meepleville is the perfect spot for board game lovers to gather. This venue, known for its friendly environment and vast selection, is a prime location for meeting fellow game enthusiasts. For those new to Las Vegas, Meepleville offers a welcoming atmosphere where you can dive into games and socialize, making it an excellent venue for building new connections within the gaming community. www.meepleville.com

Dice and Beans: Situated near UNLV, Dice and Beans provides a cozy setting ideal for those seeking a quieter place to enjoy board games and good food. As a newer addition to the local nerd scene, this cafe has quickly become a favorite for its intimate atmosphere and welcoming vibe. It's the perfect place for newcomers to meet other nerds in a relaxed and comfortable setting, fostering easy conversations and new friendships. (702) 749-3117

"The Nerd" Bar: The Nerd offers a unique entertainment blend, from free bowling to video games, all set in an atmosphere rich with carefully curated nerd culture paraphernalia. This distinctive venue attracts a diverse crowd, making it a fantastic place for those new to the city to immerse themselves in the local community. Its unique setting and variety of entertainment options provide ample opportunities for meeting people with similar interests in a fun and engaging environment. thenerd.com

ENCORE PERFORMANCES AT RESIDENT EVENTS

In Las Vegas, residential communities often curate a calendar of events with the goal of transforming neighbors from passing ships in the night into a cohesive crew. These gatherings vary from the quaint—think summer barbecues and pool parties—to the grandiose, mirroring the city's penchant for spectacle with lavish holiday celebrations.

Attending Residents' Events: Donning the hat of an attendee at these soirees requires little more than a dash of curiosity and the willingness to engage. Whether it's a themed potluck, a community garage sale, or a group outing to a local attraction, each event serves as a chapter in your ongoing Las Vegas story, offering narratives woven from shared laughter and communal experiences. No website or virtual experience can replace the simple act of showing up and diving into the communal spirit face-to-face.

YMCA: THE SOCIAL GYMNASIUM

Amid the neon buzz and hustle of Las Vegas lies the YMCA, an institution as versatile as a Swiss Army knife, equipped to carve out a sense of belonging within its walls. Far more than a place to lift weights or attend fitness classes (though it excellently serves these functions), the YMCA operates as a community center, offering a spectrum of programs designed to fortify both body and social bonds.

Joining the YMCA: With facilities tailored to families, individuals, and seniors alike, the YMCA in Las Vegas presents an array of opportunities not just for physical health but for community engagement. Programs extend beyond the physical, including art classes, educational workshops, and group outings, embodying the ethos of holistic well-being. Membership information, detailing the full suite of what's on offer, can typically be found on the local YMCA's website, encouraging a direct visit for the most personal introduction.

THE GREAT OUTDOORS AS A SOCIAL CANVAS

Beyond the neon and noise lies a landscape that invites exploration and, in turn, companionship. Hiking clubs, cycling groups, and outdoor adventure squads regularly traverse the stunning natural beauty surrounding Las Vegas. For example, you can swing by Bass Pro Shop, snag yourself a fishing pole, and head out to the local ponds or lake. Fishing isn't just about the catch; it's about the people you meet along the way. It's a fantastic way to connect with genuine folks who share a love for the great outdoors. Who knows, the next big catch could turn out to be a lifelong friend! Engaging with hiking, fishing or other groups not only nourishes the soul but expands your social circle with fellow nature enthusiasts.

EPILOGUE: FINDING YOUR TRIBE AMIDST THE GLITTER

Embarking on the journey to find your community in Las Vegas is akin to exploring one of its famed buffets—you'll never know what delightful experiences await until you dive in. The key ingredients in this social recipe include a dash of openness, a sprinkle of proactive engagement, and, most crucially, a generous helping of genuine interest in the lives and stories of others.

As the chapter closes on our guide to navigating the social landscapes of Las Vegas, remember that every encounter, every shared laugh, and every new connection is a step towards transforming a city of strangers into a community of friends. In Las Vegas, a place where dreams are chased with relentless fervor, finding your tribe is perhaps the most rewarding gamble of all. Here's to the beginning of your journey—not just to a new location, but to new friendships, shared experiences, and the warmth of community in a city that truly never sleeps.

16. OUTDOOR ACTIVITIES AND SPORTS

Forget the clinking slot machines and flashing roulette wheels, folks. Las Vegas is more than just a 24-hour carnival of neon and debauchery. Beneath the glitz and glamour lies a hidden oasis of outdoor adventures and sporting spirit, where adrenaline pumps faster than the Bellagio fountains and camaraderie trumps the clinking of cocktail glasses. So, ditch the designer sunglasses and grab your hiking boots, because this chapter is all about embracing the wild side of Vegas, from scaling sandstone cliffs to cheering on hometown heroes.

THE GREAT OUTDOORS: VEGAS'S WILD SIDE

Beneath the luminescent glow lies a world of outdoor opportunities, where nature extends an invitation to explore realms beyond the reach of Las Vegas's electric embrace.

Red Rock Canyon: Just a stone's throw from the buzzing city center lies Red Rock Canyon, a sprawling conservation area that serves as a stark reminder of the natural wonders skirting the city's edges. Its towering red cliffs and winding trails offer not just a visual feast but a haven for hikers, climbers, and those simply wishing to experience the vastness of Nevada's stunning landscapes. Walking among these ancient formations, one is reminded of the earth's grandeur—which can sometimes be forgotten in the midst of the city's man-made spectacles.

Lake Mead: Dive into the cool embrace of Lake Mead, a reservoir held in the arms of the Hoover Dam, offering a refreshing respite from the Nevada heat. Here, water sports reign supreme, with opportunities for boating, fishing, and swimming, making it a favorite escape for locals and tourists alike. It's a testament to the fact that Las Vegas's thrills aren't confined to indoor arenas—some require sunscreen and a life jacket.

Mount Charleston: Nestled within the Spring Mountains, Mount Charleston stands as a towering testament to the majesty of nature, just a short drive from the buzz of Las Vegas, and offering over 60 miles of hiking trails. With its highest peak reaching an astonishing 11,916 feet, hikers are rewarded with panoramic views that stretch over the city's shimmer to the vast expanse of the surrounding desert. The mountain's cooler temperatures provide a welcome respite from the relentless heat of the valley, making it an all-season retreat for those looking to ski, snowboard, or simply enjoy a hot cocoa with a view in the colder months.

The Colorado River: Winding its way through the rugged terrain, the Colorado River beckons adventurers and thrill-seekers alike with the promise of heart-pounding whitewater rafting experiences. Rapids ranging from the gentle flows of Class I to the adrenaline-churning turbulence of Class IV provide challenges tailored to all skill levels. Rafting down the Colorado is more than just an adventure; it's a shared experience, where bonds are forged amidst the splash of oars and the roar of the river.

VEGAS TEE PARTY: A GOLFING GAMBLE

For those who prefer the swish of a golf club to the pull of a slot machine lever (or simply want to mix up their game), the golfing scene in Vegas is as varied and inviting as the buffet at the Bellagio, with options to suit the thrifty and the extravagant alike.

Many courses in Vegas extend a warm hand of welcome to Nevada residents with discounted rates. For the more dedicated among us, memberships can offer not just savings on the green fees but also a sense of belonging, with additional perks like access to practice facilities and invitations to social events.

Las Vegas Paiute Golf Resort: A jewel in the desert, this resort is a pilgrimage site for the local golfing fraternity, boasting three magnificent Pete Dye-designed courses: Snow Mountain, Sun Mountain, and Wolf. Each course is a masterpiece, offering not just golf but an experience, with the Wolf course presenting a par-3 14th hole that's as infamous for its island green as it is beloved for the challenge it presents. www.lvpaiutegolf.com (800) 711-2833 (for booking specials) or (702) 395-1702 (General Manager)

Las Vegas Golf Club: The par-72, 6,319-yard, budget-friendly course is known for its forgiving layout, making it an ideal choice for golfers of all skill levels, from beginners to seasoned players. lasvegasgc.com (702) 646.3003

The Legacy Golf Club: Situated in the pulsing heart of Las Vegas, The Legacy is famed not just for its strategic Arthur Hills layout that teases and tempts with a mix of risk and reward, but also for its whimsically shaped tee boxes—spades, clubs, hearts, and diamonds—offering a uniquely Vegas take on the game. thelegacygc.com (702) 476-0090

Primm Valley Golf Club: A stone's throw from the city's hustle and bustle, this course is a haven of straightforward playability, where the promise of birdies lures golfers of all skill levels to its fairways, offering a gentle reprieve from the complexities of its counterparts. www.primmvalleygolf.com (702)679-5509

TPC Las Vegas: A course that wears its badge of hosting PGA Tour events with pride, TPC Las Vegas challenges golfers with its desert landscaping and elusive island greens, while also serving as a frequent haunt for local PGA Tour professionals looking to refine their game. tpc.com/lasvegas/contact-directions/ (702) 256-2000

Angel Park Golf Club: As the sun sets on the city, Angel Park offers a unique nocturnal golfing experience with its illuminated par-3 course, catering to those who believe that golf need not stop when the daylight does. angelpark.com (702) 254-4653

Bali Hai Golf Club: For those seeking an escape within the city, Bali Hai offers a tropical golf paradise right on the Strip, blending the allure of the game with the charm of its setting, making for a uniquely Las Vegas golfing experience. balihaigolfclub.com

WHERE ODDS AND CHEERS COLLIDE: LIVE SPORTS IN VEGAS

In the glittering heart of the desert, Las Vegas is not just a haven for casino enthusiasts and nightlife seekers but also a bustling hub for live sports events, hosting dozens of thrilling competitions every month. Las Vegas stands unique in the pantheon of cities hosting live sports events, not merely because of the volume of events it holds but due to the eclectic mix and the sheer spectacle it offers.

Unlike other cities where sports events might be confined to traditional, seasonal sports, Las Vegas casts a wider net, embracing everything from the ice-cool battles of NHL games to the desert heat of NASCAR races, the high-stakes tension of world-class boxing or UFC matches, and the innovative excitement of hosting a F1 street race through its neon-lit boulevards. This diversity ensures that on any given day, the city is alive with the fervor of fans from varied interests and backgrounds, converging in the desert for the love of sport.

For those eager to dive into this vibrant sports scene and catch a game or race, the upcoming events are always listed and updated at www.visitlasvegas.com/shows-events/sports-events

CHEERING FOR THE HOME TEAMS—A COMMUNITY UNITED

While Las Vegas's landscapes provide a playground for the solitary explorer and the adrenaline junkie, the city's sports teams offer a different kind of communal thrill, one that unites spectators in excitement and allegiance.

Vegas Golden Knights: Who would have thought that ice hockey would find a fervent fan base in the desert? The Vegas Golden Knights, the city's beloved NHL team, did just that, turning skeptics into hardcore fans since their debut. Attending a game at T-Mobile Arena is nothing short of electrifying, with the community's pride palpable in the charged atmosphere. For schedule and tickets: www.nhl.com/goldenknights

Las Vegas Raiders: The arrival of the NFL's Raiders in Las Vegas marked a new chapter in the city's sports narrative. Playing at the state-of-the-art Allegiant Stadium, the Raiders have not just brought top-tier football to the city but have also knitted themselves into the fabric of Las Vegas's community spirit. For the latest games and info: www.raiders.com

Las Vegas Aces: As the city's WNBA team, the Las Vegas Aces have brought a new dimension to the sports landscape. Their games at the Michelob Ultra Arena are a testament to the thrilling nature of professional women's basketball, with a growing fan base that reflects the city's love for diverse sports offerings.

Las Vegas Lights FC: Competing in the United Soccer League (USL), the Las Vegas FC brings the global appeal of soccer to the local community. Matches at Cashman Field transform into a dazzling carnival of spirit with the kind of zeal that could single-handedly power the city's millions of lights. For more information on the team and upcoming matches, visit their official website: www.lasvegaslightsfc.com

UNLV Rebels: The city's college sports team competes in various NCAA Division I sports. Head to Allegiant Stadium, a state-of-the-art football palace, and catch a game of the Las Vegas Raiders, the city's NFL team. Feel the energy of the Raider Nation, a passionate and loyal fan base that's known for its raucous cheers and unwavering support.

CSN Coyotes: the College of Southern Nevada supports five athletic programs: men's baseball, men's soccer, women's softball, women's volleyball, and women's soccer. Each team showcases the energy and passion of college sports, contributing significantly to the city's burgeoning sports culture.

Las Vegas Athletics: The Oakland A's, following the dazzling footsteps of the NFL's Raiders, have decided to up sticks and head to the neon-drenched oasis of Las Vegas. The A's, however won't actually grace the Las Vegas ballparks until the year 2028.

NEON AND NITRO—MOTORSPORTS IN LAS VEGAS

Las Vegas harbors an adrenaline-infused secret beyond its casinos and spectacular shows: a rich motorsport culture that could very well give the roulette wheels a run for their money. Here, amidst the desert's shimmering visage, racing enthusiasts find a paradise roaring with the sound of engines and fragrant with the scent of burning rubber.

Las Vegas Motor Speedway: At the epicenter of this petrol-scented nirvana stands the Las Vegas Motor Speedway (LVMS), a sprawling complex that's downright irresistible to any motor enthusiast—seasoned pros and hobbyists alike. A short jaunt north of the Strip, LVMS has carved its niche in the motorsport universe, offering a fleet of racing delights.

- NASCAR Events: Throughout the year, LVMS becomes a mecca for NASCAR aficionados, hosting spectacles such as the Pennzoil 400 and the South Point 400. These aren't just races; they're high-velocity dramas where the line between heroes and heartbreak is as thin as the finish line.

- NHRA Drag Racing: For those who prefer their cars to blast off like rockets, the speedway's NHRA events are a dream come true. Here, the Nevada Nationals and Four-Wide Nationals turn the track into a blur of speed, showcasing vehicles that defy the limits of acceleration.

- NASCAR Racing Experience: Ever fancied taking a NASCAR car for a spin yourself? The NASCAR Racing Experience at LVMS lets you do just that, offering a slice of the high-speed action for those brave enough to strap themselves into these mechanical beasts.

- Other Racing Events and Experiences: But why stop at NASCAR? Las Vegas's racing repertoire extends to Nitrocross, featuring motocross bikes that spend as much time in the air as on the dirt, and a variety of circuits at LVMS that cater to every racing taste, from drag strips to road courses.

- The Las Vegas Grand Prix: Just when you thought Las Vegas had played all its cards, it ups the ante with the Las Vegas Grand Prix, adding F1 to its already impressive motorsport lineup. Picture this: F1 cars racing through the neon-lit streets, a spectacle that promises to be as dazzling as any casino jackpot. In addition to 10 teams, 20 F1 cars, and 315,000 fans, the race also brings traffic congestion and accessibility challenges caused by road closures and construction. With an economic impact breezing past the

$1.2 billion mark and the rare spectacle of a live F1 race in the offing, some folks might reckon it's a bargain, akin to finding an extra chip under the blackjack table, while others might beg to differ.

EPILOGUE: THE ECHOING CHEER

In Las Vegas, the thrill of the game isn't confined to the stadium. It spills over into local bars, family living rooms, and bustling sports complexes, where fans gather, donned in team colors, hearts beating in unison with the play-by-play. This collective passion for local sports is a testament to the city's ability to come together, to find unity and identity in the triumphs and trials of its teams. Yes, it even allows you, the newcomer, to expand your social circle and find new friends.

In this city of lights, every venture into the great outdoors and every chant in the stadium stands is a reminder that Las Vegas is not just a haven for those seeking entertainment within its grand casinos but a home for explorers and sports enthusiasts alike. So, lace up your hiking boots, don your team jersey, and join the chorus of voices cheering under the Nevada sun. Las Vegas, in all its multifaceted glory, invites you to discover, to celebrate, and to belong.

17.   RETIRING IN LAS VEGAS

Ah, retirement. The golden years. The freedom to ditch the alarm clock and finally pursue those passions long simmering on the back burner. But where to spend these golden years, you ask? Picture this: turquoise pools reflecting the desert sun, endless buffets, and an infinite lineup of shows and entertainment—all within a stone's throw of your cozy condo. Yes, folks, Las Vegas, the so-called City of Sin, might just be the perfect destination for retirees seeking a life less ordinary.

ADVANTAGES FOR SILVER SURFERS:

Sunshine and Serenity: Ditch the winter blues and embrace the year-round sunshine in Vegas. Soak up some vitamin D by the pool, play a round of golf on a championship course, hike through the breathtaking Red Rock Canyon National Conservation Area... the range of activities are as boundless as the perpetual blue skies and sunny weather.

Affordability with a Spark: Las Vegas offers a surprisingly affordable cost of living compared to other major cities, and by now you've learned that Nevada boasts no state income tax—including no tax on Social Security or retirement income. Combined with the considerably lower housing costs and entertainment options, and your savings can stretch further. In addition, Vegas offers free concerts, community events, and senior discounts galore. Who says retirement has to be a budget-busting affair?

Entertainment Extravaganza: Vegas is a veritable kaleidoscope of entertainment options, that cater to every taste and fancy and go above and beyond bingo nights and shuffleboard tournaments. On any given day or night, you can catch a world-class Cirque du Soleil show, get mystified by a dazzling magic act, or immerse yourself in the sounds of a symphony orchestra. Craving a laugh? Vegas is world-renowned for its comedy clubs and rotation of top-notch comedians, who range from celebrity status to most-likely-to-succeed up-and-comers. And, of course, let's not forget the casinos, where a spin of the roulette wheel or pull on a slot machine can add excitement to the routine of any retiree.

Community and Connection: Vegas is a famous city, but it is also a vibrant, close-knit community that is incredible inclusive to seniors. Silver Sneakers programs offer fitness classes specifically designed for adults 65 and over, while numerous senior centers provide a place for socializing, playing cards, and attending lectures. Various clubs and groups cater to retirees, with options for book enthusiasts, gardeners, hikers, and more. In Vegas, you don't have to worry about feeling isolated in retirement—the city welcomes seniors with open arms and a year-long calendar bursting with exciting and engaging activities.

Caring for the Golden Years: Access to quality healthcare is a paramount consideration for retirees, and Las Vegas is well-equipped to meet this need. The city's healthcare landscape includes comprehensive care hubs like the University Medical Center, and state-of-the-art facilities like the Cleveland Clinic Lou Ruvo Center for Brain Health, renowned for its work in neurodegenerative diseases.

CONSIDERATIONS FOR THE SAVVY RETIREE:

The Neon Glare: The city's energy is exhilarating, but it can also be overwhelming. Living in a quieter neighborhood away from the Strip, or scheduling your outings during the day to avoid the peak hours, can allow you to freely choose when to engage with the excitement of the city, or submit to the serenity of a nearby neighborhood. So remember, you can dip your toes into the Vegas experience at will and decide when—and if— you want to take the full plunge.

Desert Heat: Summer in Vegas is scorching, probably unlike what you're used to, so it's important to familiarize yourself with the extreme temperatures and adapt to them like a true local. Pick your favorite air-conditioned destinations and poolside locations during the hottest months, and plan ahead for outdoor activities. If you're a sun worshiper, for example, embrace the early mornings and late afternoons for spending time outside.

Dryness and Dust: The desert climate can be dry and dusty, especially during the windy months. Easily adapt by keeping sunscreen and sunglasses handy, and invest in a good humidifier for your home.

Transportation Options: While public transportation is improving, Vegas is still a car-centric city. When deciding where to live, consider your transportation needs and whether you're comfortable driving or will need to rely on taxis, ride-sharing services, or public buses.

COMMUNITY RESOURCES FOR SILVER SURFERS:

Clark County Senior Services: Provides a variety of services and programs for seniors, including transportation assistance, home-delivered meals, and caregiver support. (702) 455-7051

City of Las Vegas Senior Services: Offers resources and information on health, wellness, and aging services for seniors in Las Vegas.
www.lasvegasnevada.gov/Government/Departments/Neighborhood-Services/Senior-Services

AARP Nevada: Provides information and advocacy for seniors in Nevada, including discounts and events. (866) 389-5652

Nevada 211: A program run by the Nevada Department of Health and Human Services and managed by Money Management International (MMI) provides a well-structured and accessible source of information about programs for seniors. www.nevada211.org/senior-services/

Senior Centers: Numerous senior centers throughout the city offer a variety of activities and social events for seniors. Contact your local community center for information. adsd.nv.gov/Resources/NevadaSeniorCenters/

EPILOGUE: LIVING THE VEGAS DREAM

Las Vegas, the city that never sleeps, can also be the city where your retirement dreams take flight. With its sunshine, serenity, and senior-friendly entertainment options, Vegas is an ideal destination for spirited silver surfers. So, pack your sunscreen, your dancing shoes, and your sense of adventure—Vegas might just be the unexpected oasis you've been searching for.

18.   DOING BUSINESS IN LAS VEGAS

Whether you're an experienced entrepreneur or a fresh-faced dreamer, Vegas might be the fertile ground where your business dreams blossom into reality. This chapter cracks open the vault of Vegas's burgeoning business scene, where ambition shimmers brighter than the lights on the Strip and opportunities spout like water from the Bellagio fountains.

A THRIVING ECOSYSTEM

Las Vegas is well-known for its daytime sun and nighttime fun, but it's also a beehive of entrepreneurial buzz, attracting diverse industries such as tech, renewable energy, healthcare, and even advanced manufacturing. Check out the numbers: the city boasts a 143.7% increase in startup employment between 2020 and 2023, proving that ambition and opportunity continue to run as hot as a good blackjack streak. So, you may be wondering: what's fueling this entrepreneurial engine?

SUN, SAND, AND TAX BREAKS

Since you asked… Vegas isn't just offering stunning sunsets and poolside perks. The city is also a veritable oasis of business-friendly policies. With no corporate income tax, no personal income tax, and no franchise tax, that business plan you scribbled on a napkin starts looking a lot less like a dreamy doodle and a lot more like a viable venture. Add to that a streamlined business registration process and a welcoming government eager to see startups flourish, and you've got a recipe for entrepreneurial success.

STATS SPEAK LOUDER THAN SLOT MACHINES

According to a 2023 Forbes report, Nevada ranks 38th in the nation for ease of starting a business—but who said entrepreneurial success should be easy? However, in the same report, it wins big on the ranking for financial accessibility and workforce, offering various incentive programs and grants for businesses creating jobs and investing in the community.

The Las Vegas Global Economic Alliance provides resources and support for businesses of all sizes, from startups to established corporations. (702) 791-0000

BEYOND THE BUFFET LINE: NETWORKING AND COLLABORATION

Las Vegas' emphasis on community extends to the business world, with a vibrant network of co-working spaces, incubators, and accelerators providing fertile ground for collaboration and idea exchange. Imagine brainstorming your next big app over coffee with fellow innovators, or pitching your sustainable fashion line to a panel of seasoned investors—all within the same building. The possibilities for cross-pollination and mutual support are endless.

- The Nevada Entrepreneur Network connects entrepreneurs with resources, events, and mentors. http://nve.network

- SCORE is the largest volunteer mentor service nationwide, offering personalized mentoring and a plethora of workshops and webinars. www.score.org/lasvegas

- StartUp Vegas is a nonprofit geared towards igniting the startup scene in Las Vegas, with workshops, networking, and collaboration opportunities aimed at cultivating a vibrant entrepreneurial ecosystem. startup.vegas

- Troesh Center for Entrepreneurship and Innovation provides advanced education, workshops, events and programs for students and aspiring entrepreneurs. entrepreneurship.unlv.edu

- Innovate.Vegas is a strategic initiative to firmly implement and maintain Las Vegas' status as a hub for technology and innovation. Its website acts as a go-to source for news, programs, workshops, access to events, information about government subsidies, and other resources for innovation and growth in the tech sector.

So, you've got the idea, the drive, and maybe even a killer elevator pitch. Now, it's time to find your Vegas headquarters. The city offers a diverse range of office spaces, from sleek high-rises overlooking the Strip to funky converted warehouses pulsating with creative energy. The choice is yours, depending on your budget, vibe, and target audience. Pro tip: think beyond the Strip—neighborhoods like Downtown and Arts District offer exciting opportunities for businesses catering to locals and seeking a unique identity.

SOLE SEARCHING IN SIN CITY: THE ZAPPOS BLUEPRINT

In the heart of Nevada, a story emerged that holds a wealth of lessons for anyone contemplating the desert winds of fortune that blow businesses towards success in Las Vegas. This saga doesn't belong to the usual suspects in Sin City, but to Zappos, the online shoe emporium that strolled into Vegas and decided it was home. The leap from humble beginnings to a celebrated enterprise is a narrative not just of business acumen, but of seizing the unique opportunities the city offers.

Why Las Vegas? Ask Zappos: Zappos' migration to Las Vegas was less about escaping San Francisco's bustling startup scene and more about embracing what Las Vegas had in store. The initial draw was practical: Las Vegas presented a more affordable base, where the costs of running an online business weren't as steep as the more traditional tech hubs. In San Francisco, high rent and operational costs can stifle growth. Las Vegas, in contrast, offered breathing room—a space where Zappos could grow without the constant pressure of overheads.

A Diverse Talent Pool: Then there was the talent, the boundless ambition and creativity, waiting to be discovered like a pair of deeply discounted designer boots. Las Vegas, with its eclectic mix of residents and a steady influx of bright-eyed newcomers, offered a diverse talent pool, and Zappos capitalized on this, building a workforce as powerful as its product lineup, all while contributing to the local economy. It was a partnership that fit like Cinderella's slipper.

A Perfect Match: The cultural synergy of Las Vegas and Zappos turned out to be perfectly aligned. Zappos wasn't looking to blend into the corporate crowd; it aimed for standout customer service infused with a sense of fun and innovation. This ethos found fertile ground in Las Vegas, a city known for pushing boundaries and redefining entertainment experiences. The cultural alignment between the city and Zappos underscored the company's success, proving that the right environment is key to cultivating a unique business identity.

The Takeaway: Zappos's story in Las Vegas teaches more than just the advantage of lower operational costs. It's about the symbiotic relationship between a city teeming with opportunities and a business ready to innovate and grow. Las Vegas stands as a testament to the idea that with the right vision and commitment, a company can flourish.

The moral of the story, dear reader, isn't that every business that sets up shop in Las Vegas will skyrocket to Zappos-level fame. However,

Zappos's journey from a fledgling startup to a multimillion-dollar powerhouse under the neon glow of Vegas makes an enticing, real-life success story. It's the tale of a city teeming with potential, ready to embrace those with the courage to think outside the (shoe) box.

EPILOGUE: BUILDING YOUR VEGAS EMPIRE

Las Vegas is flashy and fabulous, but it's also city that rewards hard work and innovation. Building a successful business takes time, dedication, and a willingness to adapt, and with the city's supportive ecosystem, tax advantages, and endless opportunities for networking and collaboration, your business dream doesn't have to be a mirage shimmering in the heat. Instead, Vegas can help you make your dream a tangible reality waiting to be built, brick by entrepreneurial brick.

So, pack up your business plan and polish your pitch; Vegas is calling, beckoning you to build your empire. Just remember, in the game of business, smart players know how to make their own luck. Go forth, entrepreneurs, and make Vegas your own—not just for play, but for making ambitious dreams a successful reality.

19.   CULTURAL ADJUSTMENTS

So, you've officially swapped your hometown skyline for the glittering landscape of Las Vegas. Congratulations! And buckle up, because you're in for a cultural shift that'll make your old life feel like a black-and-white movie compared to the technicolor extravaganza that is living Las Vegas.

SAY IT LIKE YOU MEAN IT

As a newcomer to this vibrant locale, you're embarking on an exciting journey, and there's one subtle yet crucial piece of knowledge that will help you blend in like a local from the get-go: the pronunciation of "Nevada".

In the local parlance, and indeed across the West Coast, the correct way to say the state's name is "ne-VAD-uh," with the emphasis squarely on the second syllable, rhyming with "dad." This pronunciation is your golden ticket to sounding like you've been part of the community for years, avoiding the all-too-common faux pas that can easily give away an outsider.

You might hear some folks, particularly those hailing from the East Coast, pronouncing it as "ne-VODD-uh," rhyming with "odd." They might argue, with a nod to the romantic origins of the word in Spanish, that their version is closer to the original. And that's a charming theory, but as it turns out, not quite right. The Spanish word "nevada" does indeed inspire the name, but the stressed vowel in the original Spanish is a sound that English speakers, regardless of coast, typically don't articulate in their daily speech.

This linguistic tussle might seem minor, but in Nevada, it's a matter of state pride and identity. The correct pronunciation is a badge of belonging, a way to show respect for the state's culture and history.

So, as you set out to explore the wonders of Nevada, from the glitzy allure of the city to the majestic beauty of the mountains, remember that a simple adjustment in pronunciation can be a significant step toward feeling at home.

Consider this a friendly piece of advice in your guide to navigating the social and cultural landscape of Nevada. Embracing "ne-VAD-uh" is more than just about fitting in; it's a sign of your willingness to understand and appreciate the place and its people. So remember, that second syllable rhymes with "dad"—say it with confidence, and let your Nevada adventure begin with the correctly pronounced word at your lips.

NAVIGATING THE NEON JUNGLE

Now, let's talk about the elephant in the room, or rather, the noisy, flashing assault on your senses—a sensory overload of music, lights, crowds, and pure, unadulterated spectacle. It's overwhelming, exhilarating, and undeniably Vegas. If you're feeling daunted by the whole shebang, know that the key is finding your own level of engagement. Take it in small doses if you need to, take refuges in quiet cafes and peaceful parks, and remember, you can always escape the Strip's pulsating heart for the more laid-back vibes of local neighborhoods.

But no matter how daunting it might seem, don't write off the Strip entirely. Embrace it. Explore it. Let it wash over you. Whether you're the captive audience to a star-studded performance or just people-watching on a busy Saturday night, Vegas is a living theater, and the Strip is its grand stage. So grab your popcorn (or in this case, a frozen daiquiri or mocktail of your choice) and enjoy the show.

FROM CONCRETE JUNGLES TO DESERT OASIS

No matter where you're coming from, Las Vegas throws you a curveball right out of the gate with the rhythm of the seasons. And don't forget the wind, which whisks through the canyons with the force of a poker player bluffing on that crucial final hand. Invest in a good pair of sunglasses and a desert-proof hairdo, folks, because Vegas ain't for the faint of follicle.

Speaking of deserts, you should also prepare for a dramatic shift in scenery. No more manicured lawns and towering oaks—cacti and yuccas are your new flora, and the vast expanse of the Mojave Desert is your backyard. Hiking becomes a way of life, a chance to escape the city lights and reconnect with the raw beauty of the natural world. Just remember, hydration is your mantra, sunscreen your armor, and rattlesnakes your potential—and unwelcome—dance partners. Don't say we didn't warn you!

Time, it seems, is also a flexible concept in Vegas. Schedules are fluid, deadlines negotiable, and the clock on the wall might as well be a slot machine flashing oranges, grapes, and cherries. Forget the nine-to-five grind—Vegas operates on a different rhythm, one powered by adrenaline, opportunity, and the promise of something spectacular happening after dark. This can be liberating, yes, but it can also be disorienting. Embrace the spontaneity, roll with the punches, and embrace the fact that in Vegas, flexibility is your new friend.

In contrast to cities like New York or Los Angeles, the attitude of Las Vegas locals toward tourists is notably different, partly influenced by the fact that most tourists in Las Vegas stick to the Strip. While New Yorkers might view tourists as a necessary but sometimes intrusive part of city life, often navigating around them with a brisk, no-nonsense attitude, and Angelenos might show a mix of welcoming charm and detached coolness, Las Vegas locals generally exhibit a more openly welcoming and accommodating demeanor.

This hospitality is bolstered by the tourism-focused nature of the Strip, where the interactions between locals and visitors primarily occur. The geographical separation, with tourists largely confined to commercial endeavors, rarely venturing into residential areas, allows locals to engage with the tourist scene on their own terms. Consequently, this creates a unique environment where locals can embrace and benefit from the tourist industry without it permeating their daily lives in residential neighborhoods.

FINDING YOUR TRIBE IN THE CITY OF SIN

One of the biggest cultural shifts you'll face is the sheer diversity of Vegas. It's a melting pot of cultures, backgrounds, and lifestyles, a place where retirees in floral shirts rub shoulders with families pushing strollers, and tech entrepreneurs in hoodies converse on line for coffee with drag artists in towering heels. This can be intimidating at first, but it's also what makes Vegas so unique, vibrant, and dynamic.

The key is to find your tribe(s) within the city's diverse tapestry. Explore the Arts District for its hipster hangouts and quirky galleries, head to Chinatown for a taste of dim sum and vibrant celebrations, or join a hiking group and share the thrill of scaling Red Rock Canyon with like-minded adventurers. There's a community (or two, or more) for everyone in Vegas; you just have to know where to look. Pro tips for finding exploring:

- **Local newspapers and community websites:** Look for listings of events, clubs, and groups that align with your interests. Check out the Las Vegas Review-Journal or the Las Vegas Sun for a broad range of local news, or El Tiempo if you prefer reading in Spanish..

- **Social media groups:** Facebook and Meetup offer numerous groups catering to specific interests and hobbies.

- **Volunteer opportunities:** Giving back is a great way to meet new people and make a difference in your community. Contact organizations like United Way of Southern Nevada. (702)-892-2300

LIVING VS. VISITING VEGAS: A CULTURAL KALEIDOSCOPE

Remember, becoming a true Vegas local is a journey, not a destination. There will be moments of culture clash, days when the glitz feels garish and the heat unbearable. But there will also be moments of pure magic, when you witness a breathtaking desert sunrise, discover a hidden gem of a vintage shop downtown, or share a laugh with newfound friends over a plate of delicious tacos at a hole-in-the-wall joint. These are the moments that make Vegas more than just a city of bright lights and fleeting thrills; they make it a community, a home. Here are some specific examples of adapting to the local lifestyle:

Embrace the casual dress code: Ditch the formal attire; Vegas is a city of shorts, sundresses, and flip-flops. Comfort reigns supreme, especially during the scorching summers.

Learn to navigate the Strip: Don't be afraid to ask for directions, be patient with the crowds—and look for the hidden gem of a restaurant or quirky bar that's around every corner.

Go beyond the Strip: While the Strip has its undeniable allure, make sure to explore the many other diverse neighborhoods like Downtown or Westside. Here, you'll find independent shops, eat authentic cuisine, and gaze at art in galleries that showcase local talent. These pockets of culture offer a glimpse into the multifaceted soul of the city.

Take advantage of the outdoors: Don't hibernate indoors just because it's hot. Early mornings and evenings offer perfect temperatures for strolling, hiking, biking, or simply enjoying a picnic in the park.

Embrace the spirit of spontaneity: Vegas is a city that thrives on the unexpected. Be open to trying new things, venturing off the beaten path, and saying yes to adventures you might not have considered back home. This is a new chapter of your life, after all, and you might just discover your new favorite thing.

Embrace the community: Las Vegas allows you to immerse yourself in its rich cultural offerings in myriad ways, such as savoring a steaming plate of mofongo at a neighborhood eatery; picking up a language to connect with new friends; and sampling the wares and experiences at festivals such as Cinco de Mayo or Fiestas Patrias. And don't forget that cultural exchange is a two-way street—sharing your own traditions and customs can also help foster a richer sense of community.

HOSTING UNDER THE NEON LIGHTS

Let's face it, being a local in Las Vegas means your living room might as well double as a hotel lobby. Friends, relatives, distant acquaintances, and sometimes even people you're pretty sure you've never met before, will inevitably see your proximity to the world's playground as an open invitation. And who can blame them? The allure of Las Vegas is irresistible.

But as any seasoned host knows, there's a fine line between opening your home with a warm heart and feeling like you're running a bed and breakfast without the breakfast... or the bed, depending on your setup. While some residents revel in the opportunity to show off their city, others view the influx of guests as a daunting task.

In essence, living in Las Vegas and managing a revolving door of guests is an art form. It requires a blend of honesty, preparation, and a dash of patience. But amidst the whirlwind of hosting duties, it's also a unique opportunity to share the magic of your city. After all, in a city built on spectacle and excitement, what's a little more company to the mix?

Setting the Stage for Visitation: First and foremost, it's crucial to set expectations early. Be candid about your availability and the level of hospitality you're able to extend. If your weeknights are monopolized by work or if your idea of cooking dinner involves dialing for delivery, let your guests know ahead of time. It's about managing expectations, not dampening spirits.

Boundary Setting: Remember, it's perfectly okay to communicate your limits. If the idea of playing host every other weekend sends you into a spiral of dread, it's time to draw a line in the Nevada sand. Suggest alternative visiting times or explore the idea of shorter stays. It's about finding a balance that keeps your sanity intact.

The Art of Independence: Encouraging your guests to discover Las Vegas on their own is not just a kindness to yourself but to them as well. Arm them with apps, web sites, and perhaps a list of must-see spots that include more than just the inside of a casino. Safety tips and transportation advice are also golden nuggets of information. It empowers them to have their own adventures, which, let's be honest, can make for much more interesting dinner conversation later.

Be a Beacon, Not a Tour Guide: Offering advice on where to go and what to see is one thing, but being expected to chaperone every outing is quite another. Make it clear that while you're a font of local knowledge, you won't be able to join them for every escapade. It sets a healthy precedent and reminds them that your day-to-day life doesn't always involve leisurely strolls down Fremont Street.

Group Adventures: When the stars align and you find yourself with free time, joining your guests for an outing can be immensely rewarding. Whether it's a show that's been on your list or a new restaurant opening, experiencing it together can create lasting memories and strengthen bonds. Plus, it's an excellent opportunity to show off your city through the eyes of a local.

Navigating the No-Vacancy Quandary: If the thought of transforming your pad into a pop-up B&B feels more daunting than dazzling, a dash of diplomacy and clarity is your best bet. Begin with a candid chat, explaining why your abode isn't suited for the guest gig or why your calendar is too crammed for company. Shift to playing the savvy concierge by directing them towards alternative digs. But don't ghost on the good times—suggest meeting up for dinner or catching a show together, ensuring you enjoy the camaraderie without the sleepover saga. Sprinkle in a bit of humor to ease the disappointment. Most importantly, once you've drawn your line in the Las Vegas sand, stand firm. Making sure your friends and family respect your wishes keep the good vibes rolling, guest-free.

A WORD ON CASINOS AND TEMPTATIONS

The twinkling neon oasis that is Las Vegas constantly pulsates with the seductive sounds of slot machines, the coy clinking of ice in cocktail glasses, and the fragrance of an endless array of gourmet buffets. Keeping a firm rein on one's personal peccadillos can sometimes feel like a high-stakes game of its own.

It's a place awash with temptations, from the velvet-roped VIP clubs promising a night of unparalleled revelry to the high-end shopping venues with their siren songs of luxury goods. It's a place where self-discipline can often go head-to-head with temptation, and winning requires a savvy blend of self-knowledge, willpower, and a few clever tactics up one's sleeve.

For example, while casinos are synonymous with Vegas, they're only one piece of the puzzle. As a resident, it's wise to approach them with caution. Treat gambling as occasional entertainment, not a source of income. There's a whole world of experiences waiting to be explored outside the casino walls.

Here's a digest of sage advice, presented with an appreciative nod to the collective ingenuity of those who've walked the line:

Recognize Your Weaknesses: First off, pinpoint exactly what lures you into temptation's grasp in Sin City—be it the thrill of the gamble, the allure of a frothy drink, or the glitter of the nightlife. Knowing thy enemy is half the battle.

Establish Your Boundaries: Before you dive into the revelry, plan ahead. Set a budget for how much you're willing to risk at the tables or cap the number of cocktails you'll allow yourself to order. This preemptive strike against excess can keep you from waking up with a wallet as empty as a ghost town after a gold rush.

Find Your Tribe: There's strength in numbers, especially among folks who are also dodging the pitfalls of excess. Whether it's a support group that meets in a coffee shop off the Strip or a digital forum filled with kindred spirits, camaraderie can bolster your resolve. If you're looking for more serious support, visit the official Substance Abuse and Mental Health Services Administration website, www.samhsa.gov, to find the resources you need.

Seek Out the Road Less Traveled: As you've learned in previous chapters, Las Vegas is about so much more than glitz and glamour.

It's a city rich with culture, natural beauty, and untold adventures that don't require a chip, a bet, or sometimes even a single buck. You don't have to go far to explore the side of Vegas that doesn't play the odds.

Embrace Self-Care: In the whirlwind of Vegas's temptations, don't forget to nurture your well-being via one of the city's many opportunities for self-care. Whether it's a morning walk in the desert or a meditative swim at sunset, attending to your personal wellness can help you deal with wayward desires and is an essential component of quality of life.

When in Doubt, Seek a Guide: If you find yourself in over your head, access to professional help abounds both in Las Vegas itself and online. A counselor, therapist, or support group can offer you the tools and support needed to navigate your way back to firmer ground.

Mind the Fallout: While this doesn't always work for everyone, it's often said that keeping the potential repercussions of a spree at the forefront of your mind—a depleted bank account, health woes, or frayed relationships—can act as a powerful anchor, keeping you moored in the face of temptation.

EPILOGUE: EMBRACING THE VEGAS VIBE

Remember, adapting to a new city takes time and patience. There will be bumps along the road, moments of culture shock, and days when you miss the familiar. But if you embrace the unique rhythms of Vegas, connect with its diverse communities, and allow yourself to be surprised by its hidden gems, you might just find yourself realizing that you've been home all along.

Welcome to Vegas, newcomers! Now, go forth and make it your own oasis.

20.   USEFUL CONTACTS AND RESOURCES

So, you've settled into your carefully chosen digs, mastered the art of navigating the Strip, and have come to appreciate the prickly charm of a desert sunrise. Congratulations, you're officially a Vegas local! But hold your horses, pardner, there's still one crucial skill to master: conquering the administrative jungle. Bookmark this chapter, which will serve as a one-stop shop to the maze of phone numbers, emergency hotlines, and helpful resources that make up the city's bureaucratic labyrinth.

NUMBERS TO KNOW: YOUR EMERGENCY LIFELINE

First things first, let's ensure your safety and peace of mind. These are the numbers you'll hopefully never need, but should the desert winds of fate send tumbleweeds of trouble your way, knowing who to call can make all the difference.

- 911: For all emergencies, fire, police, and medical assistance, do not hesitate to dial if needed.

- Non-Emergency Police Line: (702) 795-3111. This is for non-emergency matters, like reporting a neighbor who routinely practices tap-dancing at 3 AM.

- Poison Control Center: 1-800-222-1222. Whether it's a food-induced fail or accidental sequin-swallowing, Poison Control is there for you.

- Roadside Assistance: AAA—1-800-AAA-HELP (222-4357). Don't get stranded in the desert with nothing but a deck of cards and a dream—call Triple A.

- Clark County Animal Control: (702) 455-7710. For animal protection and safety issues, such as roving roadrunners or how to apply for that Vegas necessity, the Exotic-Wild Permit.

UTILITIES: KEEPING THE LIGHTS ON AND THE WATER FLOWING

Now, to the nitty-gritty—keeping your life running smoothly. These are the folks you'll be thanking (or politely reminding) when the fridge decides to retire early or the internet connection throws a tantrum.

- NV Energy (Previously Nevada Power): www.nvenergy.com

- (775) 834-4444. Keep your own personal neon lights shining bright.

- Southwest Gas Corporation: www.swgas.com 877-860-6020. Because even desert digs deserve the comfort of hot water.

- Las Vegas Valley Water District: www.lvvwd.com

- 702-870-4194. Remember, in the desert, every drop counts—so be water-wise.

- Trash and Recycling: locator.wastebits.com Each neighborhood has its own designated collection schedule. Contact your local community center or city website for details.

- Internet Providers: Pick your poison—Cox Communications www.cox.com/residential 1-800-234-3993, CenturyLink www.getcenturylink.com 1-855-550-2194, or one of the numerous smaller providers.

ADMINISTRATIVE ALLIES: TAMING THE PAPER TIGER

From registering your car to navigating the tax maze, these are the friends in high (or not-so-high) places who can help you conquer the bureaucratic beast.

- Nevada Department of Motor Vehicles: The lines could rival the Bellagio buffet on a Sunday, but keep your eye on the prize—a valid driver's license is your ticket to exploring the vast beauty of the Mojave Desert. dmv.nv.gov

- Nevada Treasurer's Office: (702) 486-4140. No state income tax is a Vegas perk, but understanding property taxes and other levies is still crucial. Don't end up owing your entire casino jackpot because you couldn't decipher a tax form.

- Internal Revenue Service: (702) 868-5005. Yes, even in Vegas, Uncle Sam can come a-knocking. But fear not—the IRS has a local office to help you navigate the tax labyrinth.

BEYOND THE BASICS: RESOURCES FOR A RICHER LIFE

Now that the essentials are covered, let's explore the treasure trove of resources that can enrich your Vegas experience.

- Las Vegas Library District: (702) 734-READ [7323]. Books, audiobooks, and DVDs, oh my! Check out the latest bestseller, learn new skills, or simply escape the desert heat in one of the many welcoming branches.

- Clark County Parks and Recreation Department: (702) 455-8200. Get your desert legs pumping! Discover miles of hiking trails, take a dip in a community pool, join a fitness class, or explore myriad other recreational possibilities.

- Nevada Division of Museums, Arts, and Culture: (775) 687-7340. From world-class art museums to quirky roadside attractions, Nevada's cultural landscape is surprisingly diverse. Dive in and discover hidden treasures beyond the Strip.

- Las Vegas Philharmonic Orchestra: (702) 258-5438. Treat your ears to the symphony of classical music at the Smith Center for the Performing Arts, located in Downtown Las Vegas' Symphony Park; catch a special pops concert under the desert stars; and explore the Philharmonic's exhibits and educational programming,

- UNLV Libraries: 702-895-2111. Looking to research that killer business idea, or go down a historical rabbit hole? UNLV's libraries offer a wealth of resources and a quiet escape from the neon din.

- Bonus Tip: Check out the city's official website for a comprehensive list of local resources, community events, and helpful information. (lasvegasnevada.gov)

EPILOGUE: WHO'S WHO

As you embrace life in Las Vegas, let this guide be a beacon that lights your way as you manage the essentials. This will allow you to fully immerse yourself in the excitement, opportunity, and adventure that define living in this dynamic city. Welcome to Las Vegas—a place where every day is a discovery and every night promises new delights.

FINDING A PLACE TO CALL HOME

1. **Create a Relocation Timeline:** Moving is like planning a trip to the moon, only with more paperwork. Start two months out if renting, at least three months if buying.

2. **Research Neighborhoods:** You've learned that there's a lot more to Vegas than just the Strip. Explore lesser-known but exciting neighborhoods like Downtown, Summerlin or Henderson.

3. **Set a Realistic Budget:** Remember, the house always wins—don't gamble with your rent or mortgage.

4. **Consider Your Lifestyle:** Are you a night owl, nature lover, swimming pool enthusiast—or an adventurous (and tireless) combination of all three?

5. **Visit Potential Homes:** Pictures are deceiving. That "spacious" apartment you see online might just be the trickery of a wide-angle lens.

6. **Check for Amenities:** Gym, pool, proximity to a good coffee shop—priorities vary, so make sure your specific needs will be met.

7. **Understand the Lease or Buying Terms:** This is obviously an important step in the relocation process, so read the fine print, or find someone who can.

8. **Plan for Transportation:** Check the commute time to work during the rush hour. If you hate driving, make sure your new place is near public transit or in walking (or biking) distance.

9. **Inspect for Comfort and Safety:** Does your new domicile have a working AC? Vegas summers are not a joke.

10. **Prepare Personal Finance Paperwork:** As with any legit move, you will need to show documentation such as paystubs, bank statements, a credit score, and more.

PRE-MOVE PREPARATIONS

1. **Budgeting for the Move**: Don't roll the dice when it comes to putting money away for the move. Know the numbers and keep your wallet in check.

2. **Hire a Reliable Moving Company**: Choose your moving company like you would choose your poker buddies— trustworthy and dependable.

3. **Inventory of Belongings:** This is best to do before a move. If it hasn't seen daylight in years, it could be garage-sale gold, ripe for re-gifting, or simply dumpster material.

4. **Gather Moving Supplies:** Boxes, tape, and bubble wrap. It'll be like the holidays, but with more swearing, and no one gets any presents.

5. **Pack Non-Essentials First**: Once you've decided what to keep, sell, re-gift, or toss, you can start packing—but leave the coffee maker for last.

6. **Label Boxes Wisely:** "Kitchen" is helpful. "Miscellaneous" is how you label a Pandora's box of future frustration.

7. **Create an Essentials Box:** Ideal for the day of the actual move, this should include snacks—moving is hungry work.

IN BETWEEN

1. **Notify Utilities:** Water, gas, electricity, internet—you know, the essentials for modern survival.

2. **Change of Address:** Alert your post-office about the move, unless you want the new tenants to receive your mail, packages, and birthday checks from Aunt Gladys (that $10 isn't gonna deposit itself!).

3. **Transfer School Records:** Ideal for if you have children or are attending school yourself, unless someone wants to repeat a grade or semester.

4. **Medical Records Transfer:** Don't wait until you have your first case of heat rash!

5. **Insurance Updates:** Home, auto, life should all be updated in accordance with your new state of residence.

POST-MOVE ACTIONS

1. **Unpack Strategically:** Start with the essentials, and leave the seasonal ornaments for if and when they ever become useful.

2. **Inspect Delivered Items:** Ensure the moving company didn't play a rousing game of catch with your family heirlooms during roadside breaks.

3. **Set Up Utilities:** Unless candlelight is your preferred ambiance—and even so, electricity and running water will eventually come in handy.

4. **Update Your GPS:** Always a good idea when exploring a new place—or, let's be honest, even just driving around your hometown.

5. **Find Healthcare Providers:** Again, it'll be prudent to meet your primary care physician *before* the onset of your first (and hopefully last) case of heat rash.

6. **Emergency Contact List:** Only the essentials, such as hospitals, the police, and a pizza place that delivers at 3 AM.

7. **Explore Public Transportation:** Take a break from driving with options such as the Monorail, the Deuce, and the Downtown Loop, a free shuttle that goes to—you guessed it—Downtown!

8. **Join a Local Community Group:** Make friends with other recent transplants or longtime Las Vegas locals, at least to have someone to complain about the heat with.

9. **Locate Essential Services:** Find the nearest supermarket, pharmacy, and a pizza place that delivers at 3 AM.

10. **Update Pet Registrations and Find a Vet**: Make sure Fido, Fluffy, and—if you got that Exotic/Wild Animal Permit—Korky the Komodo dragon all have their paperwork in order.

11. **Vehicle Registration and License Update:** It's the DMV, so bring a book... or three. And your phone. And the charger. And your Netflix password. Food. Water.

12. **Local Government Registration:** Voting, local taxes—you know, the less exciting part of adulting.

13. **Familiarize Yourself with Local Laws and Customs**: Things might be different than where you're from. Take Las Vegas municipal ordinance 10.40.030, for example: it is illegal to use swear words on the Strip. P.S. Know which laws are enforced and which aren't.

14. **Plan a Welcome Party:** Introduce yourself to the neighbors. Exchange small talk and serve hors d'oeuvres. Show them you're not a vampire (unless you are; then make sure to schedule the festivities for after sundown).

15. **Relax and Explore Your New Home:** You did it! You're home. Now comes the fun part: settling in, finding your favorite spots, and building a routine in your brand-new enclave.

EPILOGUE: DO IT YOUR WAY

As we draw the curtain on this guide to relocating to Las Vegas, I'm inclined to share a few personal musings, reflecting on the whirlwind journey that's unfolded.

Moving to Las Vegas has sometimes felt like volunteering for a magic trick, where you're not quite sure if you'll end up sawed in half or miraculously unscathed. It's a city that constantly oscillates between the surreal and the superlative, making every day feel like an improvisation on the theme of life itself.

In the time that I've spent exploring this city, from the iconic and spectacular Strip to the quiet, cactus-strewn suburbs, I've come to a few conclusions. Firstly, Las Vegas is much like a slot machine in human form—loud, bright, and with potentially big rewards for those willing to take a chance. Secondly, the desert, once considered a mere backdrop to the city's theatrics, is actually a vast stage for nature's own production, complete with dramatic sunsets and a cast of flora and fauna that thrive in this scorched-seeming earth with its secret groundwater supply. Thirdly, much like that groundwater, Las Vegas runs way deeper than its glitzy surface, offering residents and visitors alike diverse cultural experiences, community, and genuine warmth. This generous spirit and genuine connections showcase how everyone is welcome in Vegas—making it a truly special place to call home.

Learning to navigate life in Las Vegas has sometimes required a certain flexibility. But you learn to adapt, to embrace the unexpected, whether it's a sudden dust storm that has you running into the nearest mini-mall, an unexpected road closure that turns your commute into an impromptu adventure, or finding that your favorite coffee shop has been replaced overnight by a high-end boutique selling designer dog booties. These surprises—some welcome, some not—are all part of the city's charm and its relentless pursuit of the new, the now, the next.

The community here, much like a well-mixed cocktail, is a blend of history and forward-thinking, the ephemeral and the steadfast. People from all walks of life converge in this desert oasis, each seeking their own version of the American Dream—or at the very least, a table at a decent brunch spot. It's in these interactions, these shared experiences of the city's whimsy, that you find the true heart of Las Vegas. It beats not to the rhythm of slot machines, after all, but to the collective pulse of its inhabitants, each with their own individual melodies, and coming together to create a harmonious and utterly unique urban experience.

And so, as we close this chapter on moving to—and living in—Las Vegas, I'm reminded of the words of writer and poet Bret Harte: "The only sure thing about luck is that it will change." A city in perpetual flux, Las Vegas embodies this sentiment, always reinventing itself for the next act. For those of us lucky enough to call it home, even if temporarily, it's a reminder to roll with the punches, to savor the spectacle, and perhaps most importantly, to always bet on yourself.

In the end, Las Vegas is not just a destination; it's a journey, a continuous roll of the dice. May your odds be ever in your favor, and may your Las Vegas story be one for the books. Here's to the adventure, the uncertainty, and to finding your place in this glittering desert oasis.

Welcome home.

Made in United States
Cleveland, OH
21 February 2026

33677514R00105